ACKNOWLEDGMENTS

We would like to express our special thanks to Maurice C. Hakim, with whom the idea for this book originated. His insights and direction throughout the project have been immensely valuable.

We would also like to thank Dan Johnson and others at Simon and Schuster for their wisdom and kind friendship, Eddie Jaffe and Pepe Romero for their tireless efforts in tracking down the most obscure people and distant events, and Joan Raines for being far more than just an agent.

L.P.
W.H.S.

MARILYN MONROE CONFIDENTIAL

1

It was late October 1957.

I had never been more nervous in my life. To begin with, I was late. The morning rush hour had turned Second Avenue into a parking lot; I had gotten off the bus and continued on foot downtown toward Fifty-seventh Street. Walking wasn't that much easier, with stalled traffic and stalling schoolchildren providing an innocent but annoying obstacle course.

I fought my way east to First Avenue. In the late fifties, New York's Upper East Side had not yet been invaded by high rises and singles bars. My neighborhood in the East Seventies was a real melting pot, with small apartment houses and brownstones filled with plain working people from all over the world, from Czechs to Chinese.

As I hurried through the Queensboro Bridge underpass out onto First Avenue and Fifty-ninth Street, I immediately felt like a trespasser. The bridge,

in a way, divided two worlds. The *salumerias,
wursthausen,* and paprika shops had vanished. Now,
all of a sudden, there were fancy florists, elegant
perfume stores, and prim markets where white-coated
captains sold such delicacies as quail, truffles, and
caviar. This was not my world. This was Sutton Place,
the world of the rich, powerful, and famous.

I was a total stranger here. And a late one at that.
But what was really making me so breathless was what I
was late for. I had a job interview with the most
famous person of them all—Marilyn Monroe. My husband and I loved her movies. Even my brothers in
Italy had written that she was their favorite star. It was
hard to believe that I might have a chance to work for
her.

My last job had been with a lovely Park Avenue
family, but it didn't fulfill many fantasies. Like the
other quietly rich doctors, lawyers, and bankers who
populated the avenue, these people led perfectly ordered yet unglamorous lives. I was one of the support
staff who made these ordered lives what they were.

My employer was a wealthy woman who had three
daughters of coming-out age. For several years, I was
their wardrobe mistress, making sure each would be
the belle of whatever ball she would be attending, and
that during the day, none would be embarrassed if the
Town & Country photographer happened to stop by.
Elegance that may have looked casual was actually
very calculated, a full-time job for me. But now the
balls were over. The girls had packed up their expensive clothes and gone off to colleges like Vassar and
Smith. Consequently, I went back to the employment
agency where I had gotten this last job, to apply for
another.

This time, however, I decided to be a little bold. I
asked the elderly lady who managed the agency if

there was an opening with someone "interesting." I hoped she wouldn't be insulted that I wanted something other than her Social Register clientele. Park Avenue was fine, but this was New York, where so many of the world's most fascinating people lived. I simply wanted some excitement in my work. Had I been an older woman, a sedate Park Avenue position would have been a seamstress's dream. But I was barely thirty, with lots of energy and the crazy idea that work might sometimes be fun.

The minute I used the word "interesting," the manager's normally dour face lit up.

"Interesting. Yes, indeed!" she exclaimed. "I have a famous movie star for you."

"Who?" I pressed eagerly.

"Marilyn Monroe."

I didn't believe her. "You're kidding me."

"You said 'interesting,' didn't you? Miss Monroe is looking for a personal maid and wardrobe mistress. Your qualifications are perfect for her. And the pay is excellent." She paused. Her face turned serious again. "But I must warn you—interesting and easy aren't the same thing. She's *very* difficult. I'm having an impossible time filling this job."

"I'd like to try," I said, without even thinking. Anything to break the genteel monotony that I had known. Besides, I had read about Marilyn Monroe's marriage to Arthur Miller, the famous playwright. The Queen of Hollywood and the King of Broadway. Their apartment was sure to be filled with all kinds of celebrities. There would be great parties, interesting guests, all the people I had read about and seen in the movies. How bad could the job be? It was certainly worth an interview.

With all these thoughts racing through my mind, I turned left from First Avenue into the great canyon of

East Fifty-seventh Street. Towering, forbidding red-brick luxury apartment houses lined both sides of the nearly empty thoroughfare down to Sutton Place, with its beautiful private town houses overlooking the East River. Dog walkers, uniformed governesses, and elegantly dressed men and women strolled about. The roar of First Avenue had now become an eerie quiet. All I could hear was my heart pounding as I approached the awning that read 444.

A reserved, white-gloved doorman met me. When I told him I was there to meet Miss Monroe, he looked me over carefully and asked me to wait inside the entry as he rang upstairs to make sure I was expected. While I awaited my clearance, I noted that the foyer was tiny compared to the palatial lobbies I had seen up the block. Hardly the place for a big star to make dramatic entrances and exits. Upstairs, I was sure, must be Shangri-la.

My approval squawked over the house phone. The doorman ushered me to a wood-paneled elevator and another white-gloved attendant who whisked me upward. We stopped at the thirteenth floor. Thirteen! Very odd, as New York realtors are normally superstitious and skip this supposedly bad omen in numbering their landings. I hoped it wouldn't bring me bad luck.

The elevatorman led me out of the lift into a gloomy, gray hallway which connected the floor's two apartments. There was an immediate sense of claustrophobia, of being trapped in a submarine. He rang the bell of apartment 13E. Expecting the famous blonde goddess to greet me, I was caught off guard when the door swung open and I saw only a trim, silver-haired woman in her late fifties, dressed in gray. With an intimidating glare that was strictly business, she reminded me of the lady villains that you see in spy movies and murder mysteries.

"Are you Lena Pepitone?" she asked. I nodded. "We've been waiting for you." The elevator door closed behind me. I was more scared than ever, but there was no turning back. The lady did not bother to introduce herself. I soon learned that she was May Reis, Marilyn's private secretary and manager of the household. I didn't have a chance to notice the apartment, as May Reis marched me into her dark office, filled with file cabinets and a desk. Everything about the room was neat. A row of perfectly sharpened pencils, all of identical length, lay on the desk.

May Reis looked over two reference letters I had brought, and posed a few questions about my background, sewing skills, and willingness to work long hours. Otherwise, she asked me very little and told me even less. I immediately worried that someone else had already gotten the job and that she was simply going through the motions as a courtesy to my agency. However, before I had completely given up hope, a figure stumbled through the office doorway. It was Marilyn. Totally nude.

"Ex-*cuse* me," she squealed. It was an apology I was to hear a thousand times. You see, Marilyn simply didn't like to wear clothes, *any* clothes, around the house.

"Don't worry. We're all women here," I blurted out instinctively, before she could dash away. My comment seemed to hold her. She looked puzzled as to why I was there.

"This is Lena Pepitone, the girl from the agency," May Reis said. Marilyn's hands and legs relaxed. At ease with her own nakedness, she stood and stared at me dazedly.

"Oh." Marilyn hesitated. "Oh, yes. Are you the girl who's going to help me?" The emphasis was on "help."

"I hope so," I replied, my fingers crossed.

"Come with me." Marilyn gently took my hand and led me into the living room. She kept looking at me, and I looked just as hard. She was anything but what I had expected. Her blonde hair, which appeared unwashed, was a tangle. Without makeup, she was pale and tired-looking. Her celebrated figure seemed more overweight than voluptuous.

Still, she was very pretty, naturally pretty. And she *was* Marilyn Monroe. The real thing. There was something regal about her. As she sprawled on a white couch, she brought to mind a deluxe prostitute on the morning after a busy night in a plush bordello, the kind my brothers used to whisper about when we were growing up in Naples. She had an especially sensuous glow, one that could draw men to her without her having to make the slightest effort. Yet at the same time, she seemed innocent and almost helpless. Maybe that's why women liked her, too. But more than anything, Marilyn seemed bored.

Her surroundings certainly weren't anything to get excited about. The large living room where we sat was a far cry from *House Beautiful*. It seemed half-finished, half-furnished, and reminded me of a hotel. There was a white piano, some nondescript white sofas, and wall-to-wall white carpeting marred by many stains. The view of the buildings across the street was gloomy. Floor-to-ceiling mirrors were everywhere. Even the dining alcove at the rear of the living room had a table with a mirrored top. All these mirrors didn't cheer things up. The best thing they had to reflect was Marilyn.

No sooner had Marilyn and I sat down than she cried out, "May! May!" In an instant, May Reis shuttled in with a large glass of tomato juice, then shuttled out. She was like a robot. All her movements seemed stiff, mechanical, and carefully programmed.

"Tomato juice is good in the morning," I said, nervously trying to make conversation.

Marilyn giggled naughtily. "It's a Bloody Mary." We smiled at each other like two mischievous school-girls. But she didn't offer me a drink. Instead, she asked, "What can you do for me?" The question was definitely not meant to put me on the spot. Her tone was really one of near desperation. I noticed a ragged pile of skirts and blouses on the piano bench. The disarray contrasted sharply with May Reis's neat-as-a-pin office.

"I can take care of your clothes," I volunteered.

"Could you do that for me? That would be wonderful," said Marilyn in an excited, childish whisper. She took a long swallow of her Bloody Mary. "What's your name again? I'm sorry. I'm just awful with names. Sometimes I can't even remember my own," she said with a sheepish grin.

"Lena Pepitone."

"Gee, what a pretty name. You're Italian."

"Right. Italian," I replied.

"Oh, I *love* Italians," she swooned. "I was married to an Italian guy."

"I know. Joe DiMaggio."

"Hey, you know about him, too," Marilyn said.

"Sure. Everybody does." Of course, the whole world knew about the Yankee Clipper.

When he had married Marilyn, he was even more famous than she was. After Babe Ruth, Joe DiMaggio was the greatest baseball player the New York Yankees ever had. He was a genuine star, one of the biggest of all time. When he and Marilyn met, she was just becoming an important movie figure, but their marriage let the whole world know who she was. Like the Miller marriage it was something of a storybook romance—the King of Baseball and the Beauty Queen

of Hollywood, and though it did not last long, I always
thought of Joe and Marilyn together, and so did
everyone else I knew. "Joe . . ." Marilyn muttered to
herself. "Joe." She stared mournfully out of the window, almost in a trance. Later I would learn how
important the Yankee Clipper still was in Marilyn's
existence. For now, I just remarked to myself that
Marilyn seemed sincerely modest about Joe DiMaggio
and about herself, as if she were unaware of her own
fame.

"May!" Snapping out of her daydream, Marilyn
had gulped down her drink and wanted another. Again
May Reis repeated her drink routine, appearing and
disappearing without saying a word. She never even
looked at me. Marilyn guzzled her breakfast cocktail
and curled up like a contented cat.

"Joe used to take me for the best Italian dinners. I
love Italian food." There was a long pause. "Do you
know how to cook?"

I answered by describing my lasagna recipe. It
brought a hungry smile to her face.

"Could you . . ." She hesitated again. "Could you
cook for me?"

"Why not? I love to cook."

"Can you start now?" She was serious. It was the
quickest job offer I had ever received. I remembered
the warning of the lady at the employment agency.
Why wasn't there a long line of people competing for
this position? Then I looked again at Marilyn and came
back to reality. She may have been a star on the
screen, but in her living room, she was a mess.
Nonetheless, she was a beautiful mess, and here I was
being offered the chance to help her. For some reason,
I also wanted to be her friend. Despite the fact that she
was one of the world's biggest movie idols, becoming
her friend didn't seem at all impossible.

"I can start tomorrow." She frowned, plainly wishing that I could begin right then. "I'd start now," I explained, "but my family is waiting for me at home. I've got lots of things I have to do for them today. They'll be really excited when I tell them about you."

"Come on." She roared with laughter. Couldn't she believe that a world of fans worshiped her? What interested her far more was my family. "Tell me, tell me," she pressed. How many children did I have? Boys or girls? How old? Did I want more? And on and on. As she pulled detail after detail from me about my husband and two young sons, she kept smiling, but I saw tears well up in her eyes. She had wealth, fame, and beauty, but she didn't have a family. It clearly hurt her.

"Ah, kids," she sighed. "That's so beautiful. That's what I'd love to have in my life. You're so lucky!"

I wasn't quite sure what to say. All I knew was that despite my reluctance to talk about myself, Marilyn wouldn't let me stop talking. I would much rather have heard about her.

"How come you're so lucky?" she pleaded, as if searching for the key to the happiness she assumed I enjoyed.

"I'm not *that* lucky."

"Yes, you are. I can tell. I bet you were happy when you were a kid. Did you grow up here in New York?"

"No, in Italy," I answered.

Marilyn sprang from her curled-up position and grabbed my hand.

"Oh, I always wanted to go there," she declared. "Please, please tell me about it."

I couldn't refuse. As she sat at rapt attention, I told her about my childhood in Naples. She showed a special interest in my father. "I bet he was handsome," Marilyn said. I nodded yes. Papa had been head of the longshoremen's guild at the great docks of Naples. In a city where shipping was the biggest business, he had a very important job. We lived in a large house full of antiques overlooking the Bay of Naples. I had gone to a convent school and at one time planned to become a nun.

No sooner had I mentioned the word "nun" than Marilyn looked down at herself and became aware that I might be very embarrassed by her nudity. She jumped up to put something on, but I assured her that she shouldn't bother. I had long ago decided against being a nun, I explained. My father had talked me out of it. He was religious, but not *that* religious. He said that I was too pretty to be a nun.

"He was right!" Marilyn exclaimed. "You're a beautiful girl."

I blushed. What a compliment, coming from the world's favorite pin up. If only my husband could have heard it.

"So then what happened?" Marilyn asked. Her curiosity had no end.

I told her how, instead of a nunnery, I went on to a special school for seamstresses. In Italy, where the formal education of women wasn't taken too seriously, I was very proud that I had the privilege of attending this school. This and other privileges ended with the war. Like most Italians, we lost everything. Yet although the war brought us much hardship and suffering, it also brought me love. I met my husband Joe, an Italian-American GI, near the close of the fighting. I came to New York to marry him in 1947.

"Your husband's name is Joe. Just like mine," Marilyn interjected.

What about Mr. Miller? I thought to myself. His

absence, both physically and in Marilyn's conscious-ness, suddenly seemed conspicuous. I didn't say any-thing. Strangely enough, while Marilyn wanted to know every detail of my life history, she remained totally silent about her own. Maybe it was too painful. Maybe she had been questioned about it too often. In any case, it wasn't my place to ask.

Marilyn seemed genuinely fascinated by my hus-band's work as an airline mechanic at Idlewild (now JFK) Airport and by my own work as a seamstress. I would have never thought that our ordinary lives would have interested someone like her, but they did.

I couldn't wait to begin my job. Funny, I felt as though she really was looking for a friend, not a servant. I liked her, and she seemed to like me. Before I knew it, two hours and many more Bloody Marys had passed. We might have talked all day had May Reis not come in to announce to Marilyn that she had an afternoon appointment that she must begin to get ready for.

"Oh, I don't want to go," Marilyn pouted.

"You must," May Reis said sternly. "The doctor's had to wait for you too many times."

"I guess I have to," Marilyn apologized. "Do you promise you'll come tomorrow? Promise?"

"I promise, Miss Monroe."

"Don't call me that. *Marilyn*. O.K.?"

"Marilyn."

She got up to see me out. Before we could reach the door to the hallway, May Reis brought Marilyn a white robe. She put it on reluctantly. There was a long good-bye, during which Marilyn asked May Reis, who was standing by impatiently, to give me a key. There was a second of hesitation, but it was clear who had the final say here.

"There," Marilyn said, putting the key in my hand.

"Now you can't have any excuse for not coming to-morrow." May Reis took the initiative and rang for the elevator. When it arrived, I shook Marilyn's hand good-bye.

"See you tomorrow," I said. Marilyn flashed her biggest smile of the day.

"We're going to be good friends," she said softly as the elevator door closed.

I felt like dancing out onto Fifty-seventh Street. I had really done it. I had the job. I had never been so happy.

The years I worked for Marilyn were to be the most interesting and rewarding of my entire life. As I came to know her, I saw what a remarkable woman she really was. Yes, she did have problems—strange habits, crazy moods, and intense frustrations everyday people just don't have to deal with. But she also had a good heart, a terrific sense of humor, and the kindest understanding of other people's troubles. She really cared—about me and about others. She understood all about troubles, because she had had so many—too many—of her own.

From her early childhood on, Marilyn had had to struggle against one obstacle after another. Everything seemed to go against her. Yet despite her problems, she wouldn't give up. She might have cried a lot, but underneath she was strong. She had a very special determination to succeed and a will to survive that made her the biggest movie star ever. To me, however, Marilyn became more than a star and more than a job. I admired her; I loved her. Marilyn was my friend.

2

The next morning, Sutton Place didn't seem threatening at all. Yesterday I had felt like a stranger; now I felt as if I belonged. Maybe it was because I had the key. I clutched it tightly as I walked to work, pausing occasionally to look at it and remind myself that this wasn't a dream.

Even the doorman seemed friendlier. Without checking upstairs first, he politely led me to the elevator. The stone-faced elevatorman of the day before was also far nicer, as he took me up to thirteen. "Good morning," he said. "And good luck with Miss Monroe." As the elevator door closed behind me, I stood alone in the thirteenth floor's dark passage.

I carefully, quietly pressed the key into the lock. It worked! I had barely opened the door when I was startled to come face to face with the gray lady, May Reis. Had she been standing guard waiting for me? "She's not up," she snapped. "You wait in the kitchen." She led me into a small kitchen where a hefty, elderly black lady was at work at the stove. The room was adequate to feed a small family, but I couldn't imagine how Marilyn could serve a big party here. There was a small, old refrigerator and no dishwasher. Without offering me even a cup of coffee, May marched out. She had made me as welcome as a burglar. Key or no key, I was afraid again.

I nervously sat down at the small kitchen table. The black lady turned around and looked at me. "Honey, you look like you've just seen a ghost. Let me give you a spot of tea. My name's Hattie."

Hattie was a cross between Aunt Jemima and an English governess from *Upstairs, Downstairs*. This odd combination stemmed from Hattie's having worked in London for a diplomatic family. Her deep Southern drawl was scattered with English phrases— "bloody," "blimy," "a spot of" and so forth. She told me that she cooked for the Millers several days a week. There was another girl who came in to clean every other day or so. "You've got the tough job," she chuckled.

Over an hour passed as Hattie puttered about the kitchen. She was busy organizing shelves and setting out dishes, pans, and food to prepare for Marilyn's breakfast. "Three poached eggs, toast, and a Bloody Mary," Hattie said. "Same thing every day, except when she doesn't get up till lunch."

May Reis reappeared. "She's up," she said. Like clockwork, Hattie immediately cracked the eggs and began poaching them. May turned to me. "She's waiting for you. Come."

I followed May through the foyer and into the bedroom wing of the apartment. "Is Lena here?" The unmistakable voice came from the first bedroom off the long corridor, with its wall-to-wall carpeting that matched the living room rug, stains included.

I turned into Marilyn's dark chamber. May stopped at the door and retreated to her study. "Miss Monroe . . ." I called out, unable to see a thing.

"You came," she said. She seemed happy to have me there but reminded me not to be formal. "Stop that Miss Monroe. Marilyn!"

As my eyes adjusted to the darkness, I was amazed to see that Marilyn's bedroom was definitely not a queen's chamber. In fact, it was all queen-size bed and little more. The room itself was tiny. The bed had no headboard. The only other furniture was a rickety gray night stand with a lamp, a small matching bureau, a little record player on the floor, and a black telephone by the bed, also on the floor. There were no paintings in the cramped, square room, only mirrors covering the entire wall behind the big bed and another wall on the left of the bed where the closets were. There were only two windows in the room, one facing the bed, the other on its right. Both windows were covered with heavy draperies.

One of the closet doors was open, revealing one long rack of slacks on top of an equally long rack of blouses. Half the items were wrinkled and falling off their hangers. Several dozen pairs of shoes, mostly flats, lay scattered in a pile on the closet floor. I had a lot of organizing ahead.

Marilyn was sprawled nude on top of the disarrayed white sheets. A gray satin quilt had fallen on the floor at the foot of the bed. She rolled around, wrapping, then unwrapping herself in the jumble of sheets. She seemed to be trying to get up, but couldn't. With her black sleeping mask, she looked like a naked, female Lone Ranger.

"Lena," she said sweetly, "could you get me my Bloody Mary? I'd rather have you bring it than May."

"I think it's coming with your breakfast."

"Now," she pleaded. "Could I have it now?" I

went back into the kitchen and took the cocktail off the breakfast tray Hattie was preparing to bring in.

"Can't wait, huh?" Hattie asked. I shrugged.

"Oh, thanks," Marilyn said. She had taken off the mask and was sitting up. She quickly gulped the drink down. "That is so-o-o good." Soon Hattie came in with the breakfast tray and placed it on the bed. Marilyn wolfed down her meal, scattering toast crumbs all over the sheets.

When I made an effort to open the curtains, Marilyn shrieked, "NO! DON'T!" Instead she switched on the lamp on the night stand, which provided the room's only illumination. "That's better. I can't stand light this early." There was no clock in the room, so I glanced at my watch. It was eleven thirty.

After Marilyn finished her breakfast, she flopped back on the mattress. I was afraid she was going back to sleep. "Well, what can I do for you today?" I really asked just to keep her awake.

"Oh, I don't know," she said sleepily.

"What about all these clothes?" I pointed at the closet.

"Ugh. That." Marilyn made a face, then grabbed a pillow and buried her head in it. Then she slowly rolled over and out of bed. The short walk to her large closet was a major effort. She pulled out a white linen dress, sleeveless, clingy, and cut low in the front. "Can you let this out? It's too tight. I'll show you." As she struggled to fit into the dress, she sensed my amazement that she was trying it on without any underwear at all.

"It might be better if . . ."

"I never wear anything underneath," she said.

"Nothing?"

"Why? Who needs it?"

I checked the seams of the dress and its lining to

see how much there was to let out. As I got closer to Marilyn, my senses immediately told me that she was a day dirtier and more unkempt than I had left her last.

I finished my measurements. There was barely enough material in the dress to cover Marilyn's backside. She wriggled out of the dress, then stood admiring herself in the mirror. She cupped her breasts with her hands, pushing them up to check their firmness. She turned several full, slow circles, using both her wall mirrors to scrutinize every angle.

"You have a beautiful figure," I complimented her. I had the feeling she was looking for praise.

"Thank you," she replied sincerely. "My ass is way too big." She glanced again at her rear and grimaced. Her slightly bulging stomach didn't seem to bother her. "They tell me men like it like that. Crazy, huh?"

"It's sexy," I answered, and we both laughed.

"I like you," Marilyn said. She returned to the closet and rummaged through those endless racks of blouses and pants. "I need something to wear today." She yanked out about ten blouses, held them up, then threw them on the floor. "I can't stand it!" she yelled. Finally, she found two beige silk blouses, nearly alike, and handed them to me to iron. She had much less trouble selecting two identical pairs of black velvet pants. She told me that she had two appointments and would come home between them to change.

Marilyn helped me carry the dress, blouses, and pants a few steps down the hall to a barely furnished second bedroom overlooking the back alley. Inside were a bed, an ironing board, and a table filled with all kinds of sewing equipment.

"This is *your* room," Marilyn said proudly. "I hope you like it." In contrast to the rest of the house, this room was spotless, and everything in it was laid out neatly. I had the feeling that Marilyn had spent the day before fixing it up for me.

"It's really nice," I thanked her.

"Great! See you in a little while. Just come in when you're finished ironing."

I returned about an hour later and found Marilyn fast asleep. Afraid to disturb her, I started to go back to my room. I ran into May Reis at the doorway. She had come to wake Marilyn up for her appointments.

"All right, all right," Marilyn said, as May begged her to get out of bed. Marilyn seemed annoyed.

"Listen, let me fix you a bath," I suggested. "That'll wake you up."

"No! I don't want a bath!" So much for that. I didn't try to sell her on what seemed to me a good idea.

"Champagne. That's what I need," she said, as if struck by a brainstorm. "Would you get it for me in the kitchen? Just ask Hattie. She knows. Thanks a lot."

Hattie gave me a knowing wink when I conveyed Marilyn's request. She opened the refrigerator to reveal a dozen small bottles of Piper Heidsieck. She also showed me a cabinet stocked with much more of the same. There was enough for a month at least.

"That is so good," Marilyn exclaimed after a long gulp. It worked; she was up in a minute. She put on the blouse and pants, which were as tight as they could be without splitting. Even if she wore a bra and panties, there would have been no room for them. In her dislike for undergarments, Marilyn was, ironically, a "liberated woman," at least in one sense, long before the first bra was burned.

"You really don't wear anything underneath?" I blurted out.

"Never," she said, in all innocence. "I hate all that stuff. It's so uncomfortable."

I wondered how comfortable her skin-clinging

clothes could be. Moving around in them, even breathing, looked difficult. She could burst out of them at any time, and many popped buttons and broken zippers proved that she must have done so rather often.

When finally dressed, Marilyn again took a few spins in front of her mirrors. Round and round she went. For someone who seemed to want to look her best, I couldn't understand why she paid so little attention to her straggly hair, so in need of washing and setting. (She didn't use makeup or perfume, either. All that mattered to her was her figure.) Then, suddenly, on about the fifth circle of inspection, she decided she didn't look right.

"Shit!" Marilyn cursed, tearing off the blouse and several buttons, too. "It's not right!" In a frenzy, she started going through the closet.

I still had the other beige silk blouse that I had ironed. As Marilyn was hysterically sweeping the hangers aside, I quickly pointed it out to her. "That's for you."

My taking charge calmed her down immediately. She fell back onto the bed, relieved. "Gee, I'm sorry," she said, tears in her eyes. "I didn't mean to act like that. These clothes make me crazy, you know. . . ."

"I don't see how anybody could figure out what to wear here," I tried to reassure her. "I'll get things organized for you, don't worry."

"Oh, Lena . . . you really are going to help me." Marilyn held her champagne to her lips.

Between another split of Piper Heidsieck and May Reis's continued prodding about the appointments, May was finally able to call for the chauffeur to take Marilyn away. Although Marilyn didn't have a limousine of her own, she used a service which provided a big car, usually a black Cadillac, and a uniformed driver whenever she needed them. Usually,

Marilyn would prefer just to take taxis. That way, she didn't have to keep anyone waiting. But for premieres or on days like today, when she had several appointments, she would use the chauffeur service. Still, Marilyn didn't look right now like the kind of person who rode around in limousines. With her uncoiffed hair hidden in a dark scarf, no makeup, and unstylish sunglasses, no one would ever have guessed that she was a great movie star.

I worked on Marilyn's clothes until she returned from the doctor, several hours later. Then, because she wanted to change for an acting class, the morning's tortured dressing process began again. I had to iron at least three more blouses before she was satisfied.

"You know that you're late again," May Reis repeated, like a broken record.

"I don't care," Marilyn snarled, hurling a blouse across the room at her. But almost instantly, like Dr. Jekyll and Mr. Hyde, she tried to explain herself to me, in the sweetest way. "I don't mean to be late. I'm just so . . . so . . . mixed up, sometimes. . . ."

My obvious sympathy seemed to annoy May Reis, who was very efficient, even if she wasn't sweet. However, May never criticized me for going along with Marilyn. Marilyn was definitely not a woman who could be pushed around. Patience was the only approach.

Eventually, she was ready to go out again. May looked worn out. But instead of pouring herself a drink, she trudged doggedly back to her files and papers. She was content for the moment because Marilyn had gotten off.

While Marilyn was gone, I spent my time sewing and ironing. The way Marilyn abused her clothes, her wardrobe needed constant attention. I did take one break for a sandwich and coffee which Hattie had prepared for me. While I was sitting at the small kitchen table, I got my very first look at Mr. Miller. He came out of the study to ask Hattie for a snack and Hattie introduced us. He simply said a polite "hello" and left. My first glimpse of him, brief as it was, gave me the impression that he was very different from Marilyn. Quiet, reserved, controlled, like a doctor or a teacher. He wore glasses, a gray, V-neck sweater, and an open-necked sport shirt. He was tall and had dark, thinning hair. Mr. Miller didn't look handsome. He didn't look athletic. He did look smart. I couldn't stop thinking about Marilyn's constant talk yesterday about Joe DiMaggio and only Joe DiMaggio. How totally opposite the two men seemed!

As she prepared a hamburger, Hattie explained that Mr. Miller worked nearly all day long in his study, off the living room. "He stays as far away as he can," Hattie whispered. "Gets up before she does and usually doesn't say two words to her all day. I don't know what that man does in that room for so long. Whenever I go in there to bring him his food, he's just sitting there, staring off into space."

"I guess writers are like that," I said.

"I just don't know. I just don't know," was all Hattie could say. "I've worked for lots of folks in my time, but none like these."

Strange, perhaps, but I couldn't say that my new job wasn't interesting. I was eager for Marilyn to return. When she arrived, around five, she dashed into her room, tore her clothes off, and fell onto the bed. "Lena, Lena," she pleaded, "get me some champagne. O.K.?"

"I really needed this," she sighed, when I returned with the small bottle. I began to pick up her clothes and hang them in the closet. She interrupted me. "Don't bother with that. You go on home now. Your little boys are waiting for you, I bet."

"I'll be glad to stay," I said.

"No. Go on. Please." I finished hanging up her blouse and wished her a nice evening. "Lena," she called as I went to get my coat, "Lena, are you sure you're going to be happy here?" She herself sounded very unsure.

"Sure. Why not?"

"Really?"

"Sure."

"I'm so glad," she smiled. "Good night."

My next month or so with Marilyn was very much the same as my first day—my sewing and ironing, her indecision and lateness. Although during this time we didn't talk much about our own separate lives, I learned a lot merely by being there near her, on the job. Soon I began to understand why Marilyn was so unsure that I'd be happy there.

First of all, Marilyn's life was incredibly monotonous for her. Her doctors' appointments (I later learned these were appointments with psychiatrists) and her acting lessons were virtually all she had to look forward to. She spent most of her time in her little bedroom, sleeping, looking at herself in the mirrors, drinking Bloody Marys or champagne, and talking on the phone, which seemed to be her greatest pleasure. Marilyn seemed to get calls from everyone in show business—famous producers, directors, lawyers, agents, and other stars who wanted to work with her. "*That* was Billy Wilder." Or "*That* was Laurence Olivier." Or "*That* was Montgomery Clift," I remember her saying excitedly.

But the calls she enjoyed the most—and talked the longest on—came from two men who were very, very special to her: Joe DiMaggio and Frank Sinatra. A call from either one could keep her smiling for hours. Aside from the phone, however, Marilyn had few interests. I never saw her read a book or a newspaper.

Once in a while she would thumb through the pictures of high-fashion models in *Vogue*. She didn't own a television, never listened to the radio.

Marilyn did seem to enjoy playing jazz and blues records on the small hi-fi set next to her bed. I remember the one song she played most often, a number called "Every Day I Have the Blues." I memorized the words because I heard them so many times. Since Marilyn's death, they have haunted me:

> Every day . . . every day I have the blues
> Every day . . . every day I have the blues
> You see me worried baby
> Because it's you I hate to lose
> Nobody loves me, nobody seems to care
> Nobody loves me, nobody seems to care
> Speaking of bad luck and trouble
> Baby you know I've had my share.

Another song, which she continually sang to herself, was "The Man I Love." One day, after having lured her into the tub with a special bubble bath, I found her standing nude, dripping wet, inside one of her closets. She was sadly humming the tune. When I came over to ask her about a dress I was letting out, I saw that she had a full-length picture of Joe DiMaggio pasted inside the closet. She was staring at it so intensely that she didn't even notice I was there. It seemed like a religious ritual for her, a ritual she repeated almost every day.

Marilyn often listened to Frank Sinatra tunes while standing dreamily in front of Joe DiMaggio's picture. One day I went into her room to hang up some clothes, but I couldn't get anywhere near the door of the big, walk-in closet. In the closet doorway stood Marilyn, naked, as usual, even though the morning was cool and damp. One of her favorite records, "All of Me," was playing on the record player near the bed, and she swayed gently from side to side in time with Sinatra's voice. She seemed to be looking at Joe's picture, but her eyes had the faraway expression I had seen in them many times when Marilyn had been unhappy. My first instinct was to scold Marilyn in a friendly way for being careless about her health, but then I noticed that a warm, velvety bathrobe lay on the bed at her fingertips. Not wanting to disturb her private thoughts, I turned to walk out of the room.

"Don't go," Marilyn said, taking me by surprise. I thought she was too wrapped up in her dreams even to notice me. "Isn't Frankie . . . Frank Sinatra good?" she asked me out of the blue.

"Sure," I replied. "I've got a lot of his records."

"Hey, he's Italian, too," she said, smiling. "My three Italians—Joe and Frankie and Lena," she laughed. "Those two guys . . . gee . . . you'd think they'd get along. They used to be pals," Marilyn reflected, her eyes focused once again on her big picture of Joe. She turned and saw that I looked confused, so she began telling me a story about the two men.

"Joe and I had this crazy thing," she began. "I mean . . . he and I really loved each other even after we split up. Maybe we shouldn't have . . . Oh, well . . . that's life." Marilyn explained that Joe didn't want her to be a movie star. He wanted her with him all the time, and resented having to give her up sometimes when she had to work on a film or talk to reporters. "He didn't like the women I played. He said they were sluts. He didn't like the actors kissing me. He didn't like my costumes. He didn't like anything about my movies," Marilyn told me. "And he *hated* all my clothes. He said they were too tight and they attracted the wrong kind of attention. When I told him

I had to dress like I did, that it was part of my job, he just said I should quit. 'I'll take care of you,' he said. 'Show business isn't any business for a girl like you.' Joe said when he was a baseball star, he got whatever he wanted, but there I was, a movie star, and the Hollywood people just pushed me around. He wanted me out."

Later on, when Marilyn and I had become even closer friends, she talked much more about Hollywood and about how it felt to be a movie star and a sex symbol. But at the time, she simply went on with her story about the breakup between Joe and Frank.

It seems that even after Marilyn and Joe had separated, they continued to go out with each other. And Joe didn't want her to see anybody else. "Even if he read in a gossip column that I had been seen with so-and-so, he'd give me a terrible time. Maybe I wasn't Mrs. DiMaggio anymore, but he still wanted me to be his girl. He acted like he was still my husband," Marilyn said. "He wanted us to get back together, but I wasn't sure. We had lots of good times, but we always ended up fighting. I had to fight with everybody at the studio, so why should I fight at home?"

Frank Sinatra and Joe were good friends at the time, and Frank evidently said some things to Joe that made him crazy with jealousy. "I'm not sure exactly what Frankie told him," Marilyn said. "He was lots better friends with Joe then than Frankie was with me. He probably just wanted to tease Joe and figured Joe wouldn't take it too seriously. I think it was something ridiculous—like I was having an affair with this *woman* from the studio. Imagine—a woman," she giggled. "That would have killed Joe, even if we had been divorced fifty years. Maybe Frankie only said it was a guy, but Joe would have thought *that* was bad. They were probably sitting around having a few drinks, and

Frankie started to joke around. He liked to joke around a lot, but Joe never did. Joe must have believed whatever Frankie told him.''

That was the big problem. Shortly thereafter, a Los Angeles private detective firm was hired to keep tabs on Marilyn. The detectives found out through Frank that Marilyn parked her car sometimes in front of an apartment building in Beverly Hills. "It was a white Cadillac convertible," Marilyn said proudly. "They couldn't miss it. It was beautiful." She told me that she had gotten the car for appearing on the Jack Benny television show. "They told me to take money instead—something about being better for taxes. But I always dreamed about having a Cadillac, so I insisted on it. That car is the only thing I miss about Hollywood." Marilyn told me that she was in the building having dinner with a woman who was on her staff at the studio. "All we were doing was eating. Real naughty," Marilyn laughed. "That Frankie!"

But it was the detectives' job to catch Marilyn doing something she wasn't supposed to be doing, so the agency formed a kind of informal search party. There was a photographer, too. The men didn't even find Marilyn at the dining table, much less in bed. They went to the wrong apartment.

Thinking they would catch Marilyn in bed with a secret lover, the raiders kicked in the door of the apartment. They rushed into the bedroom, but the only person they found was an elderly lady, all alone and fast asleep.

"Some hot tip," Marilyn said, doubled over with laughter. "When she saw those guys, she got so frightened she nearly had a nervous breakdown."

The woman sued Joe, Frank, and the detectives. The police investigated. Once again, Joe was on the front page, a place he didn't want to be.

"The only publicity he ever wanted was on the

sports page," Marilyn said. "At first, Frankie thought
the whole thing was funny as hell, but Joe never
thought it was funny. He got suspicious that Frankie
might have played a trick on him, and he blamed
Frankie for the whole thing. Joe was really upset
because everything had gone wrong. I think he even
had a fight—a real fight—with Frankie later on. Joe
was a decent guy and he knew he was a lot stronger
than Frankie. Frankie was really skinny. But Joe
couldn't stand it when anyone laughed at him, so he
probably let Frankie have it but good. That was it for
their friendship."

Marilyn told me that, even after the raid, she and
Joe often went out together. But they never again went
out with Frank as a threesome.

"I never even got mad at Joe," Marilyn said.
"How could I, with a man who loved me *that* much?
Joe was still the most important person in my life. We
just couldn't agree about what I should do with myself,
my career."

Strangely enough, after Marilyn's divorce from Joe
was finalized in 1954, Marilyn went to live at Frank
Sinatra's house until she could settle on a new place of
her own. "Frankie and I had gotten to know each
other a lot better," she said. Unlike Joe, Frank never
discouraged Marilyn in her screen ambitions. In fact,
he used all his influence to help her. "It wasn't really
anything," Marilyn said of the relationship, "but it
drove Joe crazy, plain crazy."

"Frankie had some funny ideas, too. He could be
as jealous as Joe." Marilyn told me that her habit of
wearing nothing, or very little, around the house
hadn't started here in New York. "I never liked to
wear anything." With a slightly wicked grin, Marilyn
said that as long as they were alone, Frank didn't mind
her not dressing. But whenever he had company, that
was another matter altogether. On certain evenings

when Frank had a group of friends over for poker, he told Marilyn to stay out of sight. These were all-boy gatherings. Besides, Frank was going out with other women at the time. Having Marilyn around as a friendly gesture would arouse suspicion enough, but a naked Marilyn . . .

Marilyn herself complained that she got bored sitting all alone in the bedroom. "All there was to do was drink," she said, frowning. One night, she told me, she got so drunk that she totally forgot Frank's strict orders. She absentmindedly wandered downstairs—with nothing on—to look for Frank. She said that she was lonely and just wanted to talk to him. After walking through one empty room after another, she finally cracked open the door to the smoky room where the card game was in session. Frank noticed her before anyone else had a chance to. "He hit the roof. Frankie slammed his drink down so hard he broke the glass," Marilyn said. Frank jumped up and pushed Marilyn out of view before the others could figure out exactly what was happening. "He yanked me aside and ordered me to get my 'fat ass' back upstairs. How dare I embarrass him in front of his friends? When I tried to tell him that I thought his friends would like me more than their stupid cards, I sobered up pretty fast. He looked like he was going to kill me on the spot. I ran back to the bedroom and cried for hours. Here was Frankie being so nice to me, and I let him down."

Frank's temper may have been short, but he was very quick to forgive and forget. "No one in the whole world's sweeter than Frankie. When he came back later and kissed me on the cheek, that made me feel like a million." Marilyn beamed. "From then on, I *always* dressed up for him. Whether or not anyone was coming over."

Marilyn's main regret was that Joe DiMaggio

would never be at any more of the card games. She felt guilty that she may have come between "the two greatest guys there are," men she considered her "real friends." Yet Marilyn did differentiate between the two. Frank, she emphasized, was "nothing serious." As for Joe, however, she admitted that "I never loved anyone more."

"I wish they'd get back together," Marilyn said longingly. "They both call me all the time, but I would never mention one to the other. Never." I knew Marilyn loved to hear from them both. Whenever they called, she'd lock herself in her room with a bottle of champagne, often for an hour or more, regardless of any schedule she might have set. She always seemed brighter and happier when she finished talking.

"It's funny," Marilyn said, "looking at one here, listening to the other, and *they* won't even talk. Crazy!"

"When it comes to women, nobody's crazier than Italian men," I said. "It's not even worth trying to figure them out."

"And how." "All of Me" was playing for what seemed the thousandth time. Marilyn took a last look at Joe, closed the closet door, cut off the record player, and lay down in bed. "I'm exhausted," she groaned. "Could you get me some champagne?"

I really thought a star like Marilyn would be going to Broadway openings and lots of parties. But she rarely went anywhere at night. It was not that she didn't want to. I learned this the first night I ever cooked for Marilyn, about two weeks after I started work. Hattie had a day off, and Marilyn said that she had a craving for Italian food. I had never stayed late before; I was excited that this would be my first chance to see Mr. and Mrs. Miller together, and it would also be my first chance to observe Marilyn at length outside her bedroom area. It was as if the apartment had two wings, "his" and "hers."

I prepared a simple meal of spaghetti with fresh tomato sauce, chicken cacciatore, and salad, then I set the dining room table. May Reis had gone home (she invariably arrived on the dot of nine, and departed on the dot of five). At Hattie's instructions, I got out a split of champagne for Marilyn, white wine for Mr. Miller, and I called Marilyn to dinner. I felt very awkward about disturbing Mr. Miller in his study. He never had said anything to me except "hello" since I had been there. His formality was unpleasant; it put me on edge.

I was really surprised when Mr. Miller came out of his study and thanked me warmly for cooking for them. Marilyn entered the dining room wearing a white terry-cloth robe, which, to her, was dressing for dinner. They sat at the table and ate without speaking for the longest time. Marilyn looked at her husband admiringly and longingly, as if she were dying for some attention. However, he just ate quietly and did not look at her. Finally, she broke the silence. "Arthur" (I never heard Marilyn call her husband "Darling," "Sweetheart," or anything other than his first name), "you said something about going to a movie tonight. . . . I'd love it if we could go somewhere."

"Maybe later," Arthur answered coolly. He explained that he had some work to finish. If he did, they could go out. Marilyn seemed excited by the mere possibility. After they finished dinner, with no further conversation, Mr. Miller thanked me again for the meal, returned to his study, and closed the door.

Marilyn jumped up from the table and pulled me after her into her room. I hadn't seen her this excited before.

"I think we're going out!" she exclaimed. "Help

me find something beautiful to wear." We picked out, without any difficulty, a white silk blouse and matching slacks. She began to look, for once, like the Marilyn of my fantasies. She even took the bobby pins out of her hair, and combed it until the blonde mane was rich and luxurious. She went into her bathroom and actually put on makeup, bright red lipstick, mascara, rouge. At last I saw the famous image so many fans dreamed about.

"You look wonderful," I said.

"Oh, I hope so." She raced back through the living room and knocked on Arthur's forbidding door. She came out quickly, with some of her radiance gone. "It's still maybe," she moaned; "he's not finished."

She returned to her room and passed the time with a bottle of Piper. Every time she heard a noise in the hall, she looked up anxiously, hoping it was Arthur. After an hour, she went again to the study. This time, she walked slowly, very slowly. I sensed she knew what his answer would be. Marilyn tapped quietly on the study door, then went in. In a second she came out, sobbing to herself. Her makeup was running all over her cheeks. Back in her room, she ripped her blouse off and hurled it across the room. "Shit. My life is shit," she wept. "I can't go anywhere. I'm a prisoner in this house." Kicking off her pants, she fell onto the bed, weeping uncontrollably.

I had no idea what to do.

She looked up at me through her tears. "Lena, don't stay around for me. I don't need anything. I loved the dinner. Thanks . . . and please forgive me for this."

"You'll feel better." I stroked her hair with my hand. "Try not to cry. Promise?"

"O.K. Good night," she said.

I felt worse than she did. I really wanted her to go

out. New York could be Marilyn's town, all hers. But it wasn't. I knew she worshiped Mr. Miller for his literary talent. "He's a great writer," she would always boast. But being a great writer meant a lot of hard work, and hard work meant not going out. And though she loved people and the excitement of a night on the town, Marilyn wouldn't leave Arthur for anything, even if it meant staying permanently depressed.

If Marilyn didn't have much to say to her husband, she had even less to say to anyone else. She didn't seem to have any real friends of her own. The few people who visited the apartment seemed to come for him, not her. There were his friends from Brooklyn, Hedda and Norman Rosten, who dropped by often. Mr. Rosten, a fellow writer, spent his time looking at Marilyn, but talking to Arthur. He couldn't keep his eyes off her. Mrs. Rosten couldn't keep her eyes off Marilyn's wardrobe. She loved to try on Marilyn's clothes and look at herself in the mirror. When she liked something a lot, she would often ask to borrow it. "Aw, just keep it," Marilyn would say. I think she was so grateful just to have someone new around that she would have given everything away. "She'll probably get to wear it more than I ever will," Marilyn once told me of a dress she let Mrs. Rosten have.

Then there were Mr. Miller's children from his previous marriage. Bobby and Jane would come by to see their father after school in the afternoons. But they seemed far less interested in their father's famous new wife than in the hamburgers, Cokes, candy, and other goodies Hattie stocked for them. They also loved to play with Hugo, Mr. Miller's German shepherd.

Walking Hugo was Mr. Miller's most frequent reason for leaving his study. Bobby and Jane enjoyed going along when they were visiting. So far as I could tell, Marilyn never joined them. She was fascinated and happy when the kids came to see her in her bedroom; she usually put on a robe, sometimes even pants and a shirt on these occasions. Sitting on Marilyn's bed, her arms around them, they would tell her about what they were doing in school. Still, the lure of Hattie was stronger than the lure of Marilyn, and the children, never staying very long in the bedroom, would dash off to the kitchen for more snacks.

Marilyn got the most pleasure of all from Mr. Miller's parents. She always bathed and dressed for them, was on time for them, and sat with them in the living room. The Millers treated Marilyn as part of the family, trying to teach her Yiddish expressions, asking if Hattie was cooking enough for her and Arthur, and talking about when Marilyn would have a baby, a subject that never failed to raise Marilyn's spirits. It meant so much to Marilyn that the elder Millers paid more attention to her than their own son. She really tried her hardest to be a good daughter-in-law to them. "My family is coming over," she would say glowingly whenever they were on their way to visit.

Marilyn's only completely independent relationship was with Lee and Paula Strasberg, the dramatic teachers. Lee Strasberg headed the Actors' Studio, where stars like Marlon Brando, Paul Newman, and James Dean had studied. Although I had not yet met the Strasbergs, Marilyn spent much of her nondoctor time outside the apartment with them, either at the Studio itself or their home. At the time, I wasn't sure how much of her friendship with the Strasbergs was business and how much pleasure. "I'm learning to be a serious dramatic actress," was all she would say. She said it with dead seriousness, too. In fact, it was the only thing she ever said without sort of laughing at herself. Those words, "serious dramatic actress," echoed throughout the apartment for the entire time I was with Marilyn. Eventually, they would come to haunt and torture her.

Because Marilyn had no real friends, she concentrated on herself. Her wardrobe was very important to her. Although Marilyn wasn't neat or very good at taking care of her clothes (that was my job), she loved to own nice things, especially evening dresses. It made her feel good to know that she had them, even if she never had the chance to wear them outside the apartment.

She didn't like to go out shopping, so stores were always sending her things to try on. I would advise and comment, though it was impossible for me to convince her that everything she wore was much, much too tight. Actually, her ample wardrobe was simple: black and brown velvet pants, many pairs of identical black and white checked pants, beige and white cotton and silk blouses, an endless array of spaghetti-strap dresses with plunging necklines, and a shoe store of flat Ferragamo shoes. She owned four mink coats, in brown and white, a lot of scarves—but, of course, no underwear at all. In the bathroom vanity, she stored bottles and bottles of her favorite perfume, Chanel No. 5, along with the more expensive Joy. But rarely did she ever perfume herself, let alone bathe or shower. In fact, her small bathroom didn't even have a shower curtain. Mr. Miller used a separate bathroom adjacent to the bedroom on the other side of the hall.

For someone who didn't like the tub, Marilyn spent an unusual amount of time in the bathroom. I often wondered what she could be doing in there for so long, especially since the mirrors in the bedroom were much better for admiring herself, which she liked to do. One day, thinking Marilyn was out, I went into her bathroom to straighten up, and I found her perched on the toilet, legs up, performing an elaborate ceremony with a bottle of some chemical and two toothbrushes. She was bleaching her pubic hair blonde. She shrieked with embarrassment so loudly that May Reis came in through the other bathroom door, which led to her office. May's eyes bulged out, but she discreetly exited when she saw Marilyn was all right.

I, on the other hand, was so embarrassed that I was unable to move. Both Marilyn and I were beet red. She started laughing uncontrollably. "You know my secret," she roared. "You know, it has to match my hair." I had always assumed that Marilyn was a "natural blonde," and naturally blonde all over. Now I knew better. "With all my white dresses and all, it just wouldn't look nice, to be dark down there. You could see through, you know," she said.

"Is that safe, what you're doing?"

"It's a pain in the ass," she laughed again. "It burns and sometimes I get these infections. But what else can I do?"

Two days later, I found Marilyn in bed with a big ice bag between her legs. "What's the matter?" I asked.

"It got all swollen from the bleach," she whined. "It's so sore. Ouch!" She pushed the ice bag closer to herself. A high price, I thought, to be a blonde sex goddess.

When Marilyn went to the doctor's or to the Actors' Studio, she couldn't have cared less about her appearance. But on the few occasions when Marilyn did go out on the town, to premieres and the like, she became incredibly concerned about looking her best.

The preparations would begin early in the morning with the arrival of Kenneth, the famous hairdresser. Very dapper, like a model in an ad for elegant menswear, he always brought a newspaper to read because Marilyn invariably kept him waiting for an

hour. There were never any magazines or coffee-table
books in the living room for guests to look at, and
whatever Mr. Miller read, he kept in his study.

It was usually my responsibility to wake Marilyn
with the news that Kenneth had arrived.

"That's nice," she would yawn and go right back
to sleep.

When my efforts had failed, May Reis would then
try her hand with "our Sleeping Beauty," as Hattie
called Marilyn. May almost always controlled her
temper and annoyance with Marilyn's laziness. Once,
though, she got exasperated. "Marilyn, Kenneth has a
lot of important people to see; you just can't waste his
time like this."

"I can if I want to." It was the first time I had seen
Marilyn really furious. "I pay him by the hour." May
left meekly and apologized to Kenneth, a very patient
man, for Marilyn's tardiness.

Eventually, Marilyn would get up, run a comb
through her hair and splash some water on her face,
put on her white robe, and come out to greet Kenneth.
I was surprised that she wasn't ashamed to look so
sloppy in front of such an important beauty expert.
"Hi," she would say, giving him a big kiss and smiling
alluringly. She fidgeted with her robe, teasingly flash-
ing it open and shut to distract Kenneth from the
annoyance he must have felt for having been kept
waiting. The perfect gentleman, Kenneth wasn't at all
nonplussed. He simply steered Marilyn back toward
the bathroom for a long-needed shampoo.

While Marilyn sat under her hair dryer, sipping
Piper Heidsieck, Kenneth finished reading his paper.
The real fireworks began with the styling sessions.
Sometimes, Kenneth would be there for hours, trying
one approach after another. At each new vision she

saw in her mirrors, Marilyn would scream, "I hate it, I hate it."

Eventually, Kenneth somehow achieved the day's magic formula. Once Marilyn was finally pleased with her hair, she turned to greet her makeup girl, who had driven in from Long Island in rush-hour traffic, only to be kept waiting for hours. The makeup sessions were equally agonizing. There were endless discussions over shades of lipstick and eye shadow, false eyelashes, rouge, and powder. I had to stand by at all times to register my approval. Later in the day, after the hair and face were "perfect," it was my turn to help Marilyn select clothes for the evening. Sadly, more than once Marilyn became so frustrated that she began weeping, decided not to go out at all, took some sleeping pills, and passed out. Yet when she did go out, she looked wonderful. Here was the real Marilyn Monroe. I was so proud of her, and so pleased that I had been able to help her look her best. Few women anywhere could have looked better than Marilyn when she was at her best.

Mr. Miller, stiff and somber in his tuxedo, always struck me as an awkward companion for Marilyn on these occasions. She glowed with happiness and giggled like a prom queen. Nevertheless, each was very pleased with the way the other looked, and their special combination of dignity and flamboyance made them a very striking couple. Marilyn was never happier than when she was able to go out in full regalia, and I was happy whenever she had the chance, no matter how much work was involved.

Unfortunately, there weren't that many chances. With few friends, fewer outside interests, and no movies currently in the works, Marilyn had very little to do. So like many bored people, she ate. Hattie was strictly a meat-and-potatoes American cook, but her cooking seemed to please both Mr. Miller, who often ate by himself in the study or dining room, and Marilyn. In addition to her morning eggs, Marilyn ate a lot of steaks and lamb chops. She always wanted a side dish of cottage cheese with her meat.

When Marilyn was depressed, she sat against the pillows on her bed and ate alone. She gnawed the meat off her lamb chops, and then unthinkingly dropped the greasy bones onto the bedclothes. Sometimes she even wiped her hands on the sheets before picking up her glass of champagne. After these meals, of course, the sheets had to be changed. When Marilyn had her period, I changed them several times a day. You see, Marilyn didn't like sanitary napkins any more than she liked bathtubs.

She liked Italian food. In fact, she *loved* it. My cooking became a highlight in her life: spaghetti, lasagna, sausages, and peppers were treats to her, just as candy and soda pop are to little children. Gradually, my specialties became part of her daily diet, and she even devoured cold leftovers with gusto. "Don't throw anything away," she always said. What I cooked she would eat in bed more often than not. "The Romans used to eat like you do," I said, teasing her about her big appetite and decadent manners.

I tried to teach Marilyn to eat spaghetti with a spoon *and* fork. "It's neater," I explained, showing her the Italian way of twirling the fork against the bowl of the spoon. She refused to try.

"I'm not Italian," she said, teasing me in turn as she dribbled unruly strands of pasta all over her body. Once she wrapped two long, loose noodles around her breasts. "Look at me," she howled, puffing her chest out. "This is my idea of wearing a bra."

Whatever and wherever she ate, etiquette never concerned Marilyn. Among her unpleasant habits were incessant belching and farting. I later learned that she suffered from a bad gall bladder, which may have caused her digestive troubles. However, when she was aware of it, she found her noisemaking hilarious. Mr. Miller and May Reis were too restrained to ask Marilyn to stop, but I got the feeling that they would have loved to hide in another room when the explosions began. Marilyn sometimes noticed their pained expressions, but was always more amused than embarrassed by their discomfort. A smiling "Ex-*cuse* me" was her only apology. Tears took up so much of her time that I was glad to see her laugh.

It was very easy for Marilyn to cry. Often the reason for her unhappiness was clear—Mr. Miller had ignored her, she was displeased with her appearance, or she was simply bored. Other times, she seemed to cry for no reason, and she spent many drizzly afternoons in bed, gently weeping. One day while I was cleaning, I dusted two small pictures on the night stand by her bed. One was of a pretty woman, taken many years before. The other was of Abraham Lincoln.

"Who's the lady in the picture?" I asked Marilyn. She was in a chatty mood that day.

"My mother," she replied cheerily.

"I should have guessed," I said. "You look just like her. Very pretty."

"Gee, thanks. She lives in a sanitarium in California," Marilyn said without shame. "And that's my father," she said, pointing to Abraham Lincoln. She began to laugh.

"Come on," I said, "I know who that is."

"It's my father," she insisted jokingly. "Well, actually," she continued in a less silly voice, "I don't know who my father is. My mother never told me. So *he* might as well be my father. Why not? I can pick any father I want."

"If Mr. Miller had a beard, he'd look like Lincoln," I said.

"Yeah, I know." She hesitated a long time, then her smile shattered into a million pieces. "Oh, Lena, I wish I had a father," she sobbed.

Despite her many reasons for unhappiness, Marilyn never really took her miseries out on me. She was almost always sad, yet, at the same time, she was almost always sweet. Only once in my first few weeks did she try my patience. The fight we had that day made us closer than ever before, and from then on, she began to open up to me entirely.

The trouble started when Marilyn decided, on a whim, that she wanted all her blouse collars heavily starched like the collars on men's shirts. I tried to convince her that a soft collar, which lay flat, was more feminine, more flattering to her, but she insisted on having it her way.

When I returned hours later, arms full of freshly starched and ironed blouses, Marilyn ordered me to wait. She tried on each blouse in turn, complained that its collar wasn't stiff enough, and then threw it into a pile of crumpled laundry on the floor. My heart sank as I saw all my hard work being destroyed.

"You tricked me. You did it your way, not mine! Everybody does it their way. Damn you! I'm the boss here. I pay the bills. Can't I have anything my way? My way! Hear me? MY WAY! I want it my way!" She flew into a blind rage, tore all the buttons off the blouse she had on, and tried to rip off the entire collar. Then she hurled the tattered blouse in my face. "There. Take your goddamn soft collar."

I ran out of the room, into my room, unable to hold back my tears. I wanted to quit. I began getting my things together. Within a minute, Marilyn was in my room, crying much harder than I was. "Lena, Lena, I'm sorry. Oh, I'm so sorry. Please talk to me. Don't hate me. Don't. Oh, please say something. Talk to me. I need you so much!" She threw her arms around me, and I held her close like a little baby. How could I be angry? How could anyone?

Marilyn wouldn't let me leave her room for the rest of the day. That evening when I was about to go home, she insisted on waving good-bye to me from her window. She wanted the chauffeur to take me home, but I refused. When I came out of the front door of the building and started across Fifty-seventh Street, I could hear Marilyn's voice reaching out to me from her window high above. "Lena! Lena! See you tomorrow!" She had the window open and was leaning out so far, blowing kisses, that I was afraid she might fall. I blew her a kiss, and waved her back in. From that day on, Marilyn became more than a job to me. She became my special friend, my special responsibility, a part of my family, a part of my life.

3

The little fray with Marilyn over the starched collars made her draw me closer and closer to her than ever before. The slightest possibility that she could drive me into leaving just terrified her. Now she seemed reluctant to let me go home in the evening. Every night as she waved good-bye to me from her window, she looked so apprehensive, as if she might not see me again. Of course, I wouldn't let her down. Sensing she needed me more than anyone, I even began neglecting my family for her sake.

Luckily, the Pepitone family also lived in our apartment building and could take care of my little boys as well as Joe, my husband. They were all very understanding. Whenever Marilyn asked about my babies, though, she could tell that I missed them. One day she suddenly said, "Bring them here."

"I couldn't do that."

"Why not? Please bring them. Please. I'd love that."

I knew she meant it. Perhaps she wanted a chance to play mother. It didn't matter what her reasons were, for soon I was picking up Joey and Johnny each day after school, often with Marilyn's chauffeur, to take them to Fifty-seventh Street. I felt funny riding up in a big black Cadillac; everyone probably thought we were celebrities. The boys would stay until five thirty, when Joe came to take them home. It really thrilled him to meet Marilyn. She always greeted him with a big "Hi" and a big kiss.

My boys had a wonderful time at Marilyn's. They would eat in the kitchen, bang on the piano, hide in all the closets, and, most important, play with her. Since they were so much younger than Mr. Miller's teenagers, Marilyn usually didn't bother to dress in front of them. They weren't sure exactly what they were looking at, but their big eyes told me they knew they were seeing something very different and special. A favorite game for Joey and Johnny was using Marilyn's bed as a trampoline, while she sang them Broadway songs like "I Get a Kick Out of You."

Marilyn was forever hugging and kissing the boys, asking them about school, and looking wistfully at them. Many times she broke down crying after they left. "Oh, Lena, I love them so much. I want to have babies. I do."

"You will, you will," I constantly assured her. Somehow, when the boys left, Marilyn would get particularly depressed. "I really miss them," she often said. But loneliness wasn't Marilyn's only problem. Frequently, I would come into her room and find pages of different scripts scattered all over the bed and floor, sometimes in shreds. "I can't learn this," Marilyn would be screaming. "I can't act. It won't work."

Once I saw her rip the pages out of a script and hurl them above her head, like a snowstorm. Then she'd start weeping so hard that only a heavy serving of champagne could calm her. On nights like these, I would begin staying on with her, often until after midnight. During these late evenings, with everyone gone and Mr. Miller in his study, Marilyn started to talk about what was making her unhappy.

"What am I doing in New York?" she would ask. "What the hell am I doing here?" Her tone was partly angry but mostly helpless. "Is anything going to work out?"

Because her troubled present was occupying all her thoughts, Marilyn still hadn't spoken of her distant past—her childhood, her marriages, her start in films. At this time, her first and foremost concern was to become a serious actress, instead of the sex star everyone knew her as. "I want to act. I really do." This desire, Marilyn told me, was what had brought her to Manhattan. She would say, "I had enough of all that Hollywood shit." She seemed both confused and resentful that Hollywood had built her up into this great sex symbol. "I guess I looked pretty good," she said, "but there were so many girls out there who looked better. You should see it. It's like a beauty contest. I guess I was lucky." There was a long pause, and then she added, "For a while."

"I did what they said." She spoke bitterly of the movie producers. "And all it got me was a lot of abuse. Everyone's just laughing at me. I hate it. Big breasts, big ass, big deal. Can't I be anything else? Gee, how long can you be sexy?" She would stop and look at herself in the mirror for a long time. I could sense that she was terribly afraid of getting old. "You've got to have something else."

"That *There's No Business Like Show Business*

was it. The last straw!" she raved. "That was supposed to be a big hit. And when it wasn't, who do they blame? Me! I was 'obscene.' I was a 'menace' to kids. Can you believe it?" The big musical should have been a success, she explained. It had the songs of the famous tunesmith Irving Berlin. It had the unforgettable booming voice of Ethel Merman, the star of such Broadway shows as *Annie Get Your Gun*. And it also had Marilyn. Her big number was called "Tropical Heat Wave." "I guess it was pretty hot," she smiled. "I was wearing this open skirt—I think they call it flamenco—with this black bra and panties underneath. The dance people kept making me flash the skirt wide open and jump around like I had a fever. They called it a native dance. Ha! It was ridiculous, come to think of it," she snickered. "Movies!" The number was panned by the movie critics as being incredibly dirty, and in the worst taste, mainly because of the way Marilyn wiggled when she danced, surrounded by a group of leering natives.

"Can I help it?" Marilyn pleaded. "I just did the best I could. I did what they told me to. They said it was good for me, good for the picture. Shit! Good for them, that's all. Everybody hated me after that picture. Including Joe [DiMaggio]. He was an old-fashioned guy. The only place he wanted me to be sexy was at home. With him."

Marilyn explained that Joe had absolutely no respect for Hollywood or for her Hollywood career. "He was the first one who said I shouldn't be a dumb blonde. And he hated Los Angeles, too. He was from San Francisco, and everybody from San Francisco thinks Los Angeles is horrible. Frankly, I wasn't so crazy about San Francisco. Joe's folks were real nice to me and I liked them a lot, but I got bored just hanging around their restaurant and going out on Joe's boat. And that fog! I could be plenty romantic without that fog. I just kept catching colds and then I didn't feel romantic at all. But for Joe there were only two places in the world—San Francisco and New York.''

When she signed for *There's No Business Like Show Business,* Marilyn thought she would be making a movie Joe could be proud of. It seemed to her like a screen version of a Broadway musical. After all, it would feature Broadway star Ethel Merman singing Irving Berlin hits. But even before the premiere of the film, Joe told Marilyn that it was nothing more than a cheap Hollywood exploitation of the New York stage. He had seen her notorious ''Heat Wave'' number and thought it disgraceful. When studio executives asked him to pose for publicity photos on the lot with Marilyn, Joe flatly refused. But the next day, he was more than happy to pose with Ethel Merman and Irving Berlin. ''They may have been his New York friends,'' Marilyn complained, ''but I was his wife. . . .

''He told me they were real pros. They deserved to be stars because they had real talent and had worked hard to earn their reputations. He thought that being a star just because you were pretty or sexy, well, that was cheating. 'Look at you and look at Ethel,' he yelled at me. 'What could you do on a Broadway stage?' '' Marilyn said this made her feel terrible, but that Joe hadn't meant to be cruel. He just wanted to show her that her stardom had been manufactured by the Hollywood producers. She was at their mercy; he constantly warned her. If, one day, they decided she wasn't sexy, that was the end of her career.

''He didn't believe that I had any talent to fall back on. That scared me to death. I wanted a career, and even though I couldn't act then, I sure wanted to learn.'' But Joe wanted Marilyn to forget about acting altogether. He loved her for herself, and wanted her to be his wife—full time. He was a rich man, and she didn't need a career to support herself. "He thought I was the best woman there was," Marilyn said, "but he never believed I could act. Besides, Joe said that even if I could act like Bette Davis, the studios still wouldn't give me the parts I wanted. 'You're trapped as a dumb blonde. That's it,' he said. Well, I wanted to prove myself—to him and to me."

Joe did nothing to encourage Marilyn's career. In fact, he did everything he could to slow it down. He refused to escort Marilyn to Hollywood parties, so necessary to a star's public image. The only exception to Joe's antimovie, anti-Hollywood attitude would be to take Marilyn out to dinner with his then close friend Frank Sinatra. Almost everyone else in the business was off limits. "Aside from Frankie, all Joe cared about was golf and television. That was it," Marilyn said. "And he never played with any movie people. Gee, he stayed in the house even more than Arthur. Except, he wasn't writing. Just watching television. It was like he was on strike." Marilyn said that the only time Joe would even go with her to a premiere was a year after they were divorced, and only then because she begged him to do her a favor.

Despite Joe's attitude, Marilyn was as determined as ever. "I had always been nothing, a nobody. Then I had a chance to be somebody. I couldn't give it up, just when things were looking good for me. Not just to be a housewife, even Joe's housewife. I had to see if I could be a success on my own." She hesitated. "That was then. Now when I talk to Joe and tell him what I'm going through, he just says, 'I told you,' and I keep thinking that he wasn't wrong. But, honest, I love being a star. After all I've been through, I won't quit now."

Marilyn felt that *The Seven Year Itch,* her next

movie, ruined things with Joe altogether and caused their divorce. "It was that skirt thing, you know, when the wind from the subway blew it up." Marilyn was talking about the famous scene where she was standing over a subway grating and a draft shot her skirt up over her white panties. Her co-star Tom Ewell, playing a married man whose wife is away for the summer, loved it. So did the public. Joe didn't. "Gee, imagine if they had let me dress the way I really do," she giggled wickedly, referring to her habit of never wearing panties. "Wouldn't that have been something?" She turned sad again. "So what good is being a sex star if it drives your man away?"

Even though the public was lining up at the movie box offices to see Marilyn, the few negative reviews and Joe DiMaggio's crushing criticisms left her feeling humiliated. "Here I was, supposedly becoming a star, and I was miserable. God, I felt low." It was during this depression period that Marilyn met Lee and Paula Strasberg, who apparently encouraged her to study acting with them in New York. "They thought I could be a serious dramatic actress," Marilyn said, emphasizing her favorite phrase. "They seemed so nice, I really believed them."

In addition to the kind words of the Strasbergs, Marilyn was also getting praise from a young high-fashion photographer named Milton Greene, who took pictures of her for *Look* magazine. "He had done shots of everyone, Marlene Dietrich, Grace Kelly. I was really impressed. And he was such a young guy, too," Marilyn said. "I figured he must be going places." Greene, too, felt that Marilyn could become a "serious dramatic actress," she said. He urged her to come to New York and set up a company with him; he would produce a different kind of film for her. She said he promised her that, with him, she could make a good name for herself, in good movies. Furthermore, he made her feel that, with him, she could be a success on her own terms, not those dictated by the Hollywood producers. "You'll be the producer," she said he told her. She'd never be forced into a "Tropical Heat Wave" again.

"That all sounded awfully good to me," she said. "Besides, Joe didn't want me to be a serious dramatic anything, except a wife, and I really wanted to be an actress. Some kind of actress. At least I thought I did . . . then. When we broke up, I was so confused. . . . I still am. . . . Well, anyway, I was ready to get the hell out of Hollywood. New York seemed like a new chance. . . . Oh, yeah," she added, with an after-thought, "and there was Arthur. He was here, too. So I came."

Marilyn didn't say much about Milton Greene, but what she did say always had a ring of disappointment. "He told me I never had to be a dumb blonde again. Ha! You know what I ended up being? A dumb blonde!" Marilyn said that she had hoped that Milton Greene would help her develop into an elegant, sophisticated woman, like Greene's wife, Amy, who was a model. "Amy was what I thought all New York women were like. Lots of style, class. Well, look at me now. New York didn't rub off on me, did it?"

"Most women would give anything to look like you," I assured her, because I believed it.

"Come on, Lena."

"Honest," I said. She hugged me.

Marilyn spoke about how the Greenes had let her live with them at their Connecticut home, and then how they set her up in her own suite at the Waldorf-Astoria. "At first, Milton did everything he could to make me look like a *Vogue* model . . . a fat *Vogue* model," she chuckled. "Kenneth, nail girls, makeup girls, skin girls, dressmaker, everything. I think he wanted to make me another Amy. He gave up pretty quick."

Sometimes Marilyn could joke like this about herself. Other times, she would think about what she had said and lose all the self-confidence she may have felt. "Lena, it's not funny," she would begin to sob. "What am I? What can I do? I'm nothing. Nothing." Then she would pull her legs up to her stomach on the bed, like a little baby, and sob. I would cover her up, and sit by her side until she cried herself to sleep.

A short time later, Marilyn told me about the two movies she had made with Milton Greene. She was convinced that she was nothing but a "dumb blonde" in them both. The first movie was *Bus Stop*. "It was about this crummy nightclub singer and some cowboy who falls in love with her," Marilyn said. Marilyn was proud of the fine reviews the film got, but she was even prouder of the way she sang "That Old Black Magic" in the movie. She loved to sing, and insisted on performing the number for me many times. "She was really dumb," Marilyn said of the girl she played. To Marilyn, the character was what mattered, not her own performance, no matter how well she did. She simply didn't like her roles. "I'd love to play a real lady. Just once," she said, almost pleading.

The second Greene movie, *The Prince and the Showgirl*, was one she talked endlessly about. Marilyn loved to travel and *The Prince and the Showgirl* gave her a chance to go to England. It was her second big trip abroad. The first trip had been to Japan, to promote baseball with Joe DiMaggio, and to entertain the troops in Korea. All she seemed to remember was that the Japanese were small and bowed a lot and that she was always being offered hot hand towels. What she liked most was the fact that she had gone to an exotic place.

Then, there was the new excitement of performing before a live audience. "The troops in Korea went wild for me," she would glow. "I couldn't believe it. There were thousands of them screaming for me. I was scared, but I'd do it again." She was thrilled to see live people respond to her. "I never believed all the fan mail I got was real until I sang for the troops. Wow! They really liked me." No other experience in her whole life that she ever told me about seemed to give her more self-respect than her reception by the GIs. There she sang and was herself. It was no act. But the idea of the live stage intrigued her. Her new goal now was serious acting, and she couldn't take her mind off it.

Marilyn wanted to go everywhere and anywhere. She talked about going to Italy with me. "I want to meet your family," she said over and over. "Do you think they'll like me?" When I answered her that she was their favorite star, she seemed really proud. She also complained about Mr. Miller's not wanting to go anywhere. "The government thinks he's a Communist," she said. "They'd give him a hard time about traveling, so he doesn't even try . . . but at least we got to England." I later learned that Mr. Miller was being investigated by Congress for left-wing activities in his past, when he and Marilyn were married. In moments of anger, she would take credit for getting him off the hook. "I stood up for him in public. They knew I wasn't a Communist. If it wasn't for me, Arthur wouldn't have gone anywhere."

Marilyn liked the trip to England for *The Prince and the Showgirl* but she didn't like the reception she got. "The English were supposed to be so nice, but they treated me like a freak, a sex freak." She said the British press acted like a mob of love-starved school-boys. "All they wanted to know was whether I slept without any clothes on, did I wear underwear, what were my measurements. Gosh, don't they have women in England?" Even worse, she felt slighted that the London *Times* ignored her completely, while the cheap tabloids fawned over her. For a woman who never read newspapers, her concern about newspaper status seemed odd. Nevertheless, though she generally ignored the world news, she had numerous scrapbooks of her own clippings from English papers, most of which distressed her now because of their emphasis on sex.

The whole experience was very frustrating for her, especially her relations with Sir Laurence Olivier. She thought it was a great honor to appear opposite England's leading actor but felt Sir Laurence thought it a terrible chore. "I think he hated me," Marilyn frowned. "He gave me the dirtiest looks, even when he was smiling. I was sick half the time, but he didn't believe me, or else he didn't care. On with the show, and all that, you know. I tried. Honest." Quiet tears started rolling down her cheeks, "But everyone in the movie followed him [Olivier], you know, because he was a great actor and all. So they hated me, too, cause I was late. I couldn't help it. I couldn't. You believe me, don't you, Lena?" Marilyn told me that she tried to flirt with Olivier, especially at parties when she was wearing tight, revealing gowns which she thought might have helped him overcome his English reserve. It didn't help. "He looked at me like he had just smelled a pile of dead fish. Like I was a leper, or something awful. He'd say something like, 'Oh, how simply ravishing, my dear.' But he really wanted to throw up." She was completely exasperated.

Marilyn said that the English experience made her a nervous wreck. Not only was she trying to look good for Lord Olivier but also for Mr. Miller, Milton Greene, and Paula Strasberg, who were all there for the filming. These last three were the most important figures in her life, and she wanted desperately to avoid letting them down. The pressure must have been tremendous.

Still, it was her feeling of failure in the eyes of Olivier that hurt her most. "I couldn't believe it. Here I was with the most famous actor in the whole world. I just felt like a little fool the whole time." Marilyn kept giving credit to Lord Olivier for being a marvelous performer. Since I had never seen any of his movies, I asked her to tell me about some of his most famous roles, so that I could get a little better idea of him. Marilyn gave me a blank stare. "His movies?" She had never seen any of his films, she sheepishly admitted. "I saw his wife, Scarlett O'Hara, in *Gone With the Wind*, though. She was great."

"You mean Vivien Leigh?" I asked. I had seen that movie.

Marilyn giggled. "Whatever her name was. Her Highness, Lady Olivier," she said, in a parody of a British accent. "She didn't like me either. She thought I stole her part and ruined it." Vivien Leigh had played Marilyn's showgirl in the stage version opposite her husband. Actually, Marilyn hadn't stolen the part. Milton Greene had simply bought it for her. Marilyn Monroe Productions, as their company was called, had purchased movie rights to the play called *The Sleeping Prince*. Olivier was hired to be both co-star and director. "He worked for us," Marilyn once boasted. Whatever, Marilyn reported a lot of resentment both of her and her "rich Americans" using their dollars to "buy" British artistry.

Marilyn said the whole deal backfired. Instead of turning into a Vivien Leigh, Marilyn felt that again she was just "another dumb blonde," way out of her league with all those lords and ladies. To compound the problem, most of the reviews were awful. She added Milton Greene to the long list of people who had disappointed her and she eventually broke up their company.

Marilyn believed that Mr. Greene had put his own goals as a film producer ahead of hers as an actress. What better way to get into show business than sign an exclusive contract with one of its biggest stars? All the "great actress" talk, she felt, had been just that—talk. Once the papers were signed, Mr. Greene was forced to play the game as Hollywood called the turns. "I was a sex star, and that was it. Those were the rules," she said. Dumb blondes meant smart money at the box office, and money, to Hollywood, was all that mattered. "I'm trapped," Marilyn would moan. This was business, strictly business. The system swallowed him up, too, as she saw it. Who could get her the "quality parts" she wanted, Marilyn wondered.

To Marilyn the one saving grace of *The Prince and the Showgirl* was her having the opportunity to meet Queen Elizabeth. Even if she couldn't play a queen, at least she had met one. "It was the most exciting thing that ever happened to me," Marilyn said proudly. "I really didn't know what to say to the queen. So I just curtsied. I had learned how for the movie." She roared loudly, explaining that she nearly fell over but somehow managed to keep her balance. I was so glad to see her laughing.

With Milton Greene out of the picture, the position of chief adviser and great hope passed to the Strasbergs. They, more than anyone else, were responsible for Marilyn's dream to become a real actress. A New York actress, not a Hollywood sex goddess. To Marilyn, the Strasbergs stood for Broadway, legitimacy, and integrity in the acting profession. With them her acting career could take on a dignity it had not known. She felt they wouldn't let her be "used" just to make money. "They'll never let me down," she asserted, "not for anything." I rarely saw either of the Strasbergs at the apartment, although Paula tended to come by more often than Lee. Evidently, Mr. Miller didn't get along with them that well, so Marilyn either saw them at the Actors' Studio or at their apartment on Central Park West.

The Strasbergs always frightened me. Neither ever smiled. Lee Strasberg was a small, bald man with an intense sneer. I couldn't imagine him ever saying anything nice about anyone's acting, not even Sir Laurence Olivier's. The fact that he actually praised Marilyn, embraced her, laughed with her must have meant a great deal. If Lee Strasberg said Marilyn had enormous potential, it had to be so. Or at least Marilyn thought.

Most important, Lee Strasberg represented to Marilyn everything that Hollywood lacked. Here was an *artist,* an intellectual, not a money machine. Lee, Marilyn said, had been born in Russia; his immigrant parents worked in the garment sweatshops of the Lower East Side. He had worked his way up in the theater the hard way, both as an actor and a director. He, too, had tried Hollywood, but quickly left. The fact that he had gotten out made Marilyn more secure in her own decision. Here was America's foremost acting teacher. People would do anything to study under him. And he wanted Marilyn. She was moved. In Lee, she really felt she had a white knight, although an unshaven and undashing one, to stand up for her against Hollywood bigwigs who had previously dictated her life.

Paula Strasberg was less intimidating, though anything but a fun person. Herself a former actress, she served as Marilyn's personal dramatics coach, constantly by her side, in *The Prince and the Showgirl* and other movies. "I couldn't get a line out without her," Marilyn said. "And she protects me on the set. They can't take advantage of me when she's there. With her, we do the scenes my . . . the right way. Paula's my friend." Paula's value to Marilyn, if I recall correctly what Marilyn said, was reflected in the huge salary she drew—almost $2000 a week. Paula, who usually wore dumpy old black dresses, certainly didn't spend her salary on making herself elegant. She was plain and plump, but what mattered to Marilyn was Paula's loyalty to her and constant encouragement.

Nonetheless, Marilyn still wasn't sure. "Lena, do you really think I could be on Broadway? I mean, what if I forgot my lines . . . in front of all those people?" These were typical questions she would ask, not really expecting an answer. She had other suspicions regarding money. Frequently, she mentioned that Lee Strasberg was always complaining about how little money the Studio had. It depended upon donations. After all, it was hard to be an artist and a businessman at the same time. Marilyn was the one student at the Studio who wasn't a struggling actor or actress. Could they be buttering her up just to take advantage of her stardom and wealth? she sometimes wondered. "Can I really be as good as they say? It's impossible. I don't know." She just shook her head, and stared in the mirror.

I wondered, too. In her movies, Marilyn *looked* different from the way she looked at home. But she didn't act different, or, at least, that different. She could be helpless, innocent, sexy, sweet, extremely gay or extremely sad, that was Marilyn. It wasn't a performance. Perhaps the people liked her onscreen so much because she was natural, just being herself. Trying to act according to a book, or even according to the Strasberg "Method," seemed an artificial attempt to impose order on a very human disorder that the world loved as is.

"A dumb blonde? That's all I am. Who are they kidding?" Marilyn would moan, time and again, as she tried to follow the acting programs the Strasbergs assigned her. She would often have me sit on her bed as she paced around the room, trying desperately to remember lines she would have to say in class. I would read one part, while she would forget hers. "Shit!" was her favorite curse when she failed. Sometimes Piper Heidsieck would help, but usually it made her give up and take a nap. Other times, she would simply hold a script and stare at herself in the mirror. "Get in touch with the character. Get in touch with the character," she would mime what the Strasbergs must have told her. "Get in touch! I wish you could just call the stupid character on the phone."

Marilyn had the hardest time pronouncing words. She was constantly running through her bathroom into May Reis's office to ask what something meant and how to say it correctly. For a while, she even enrolled for special English lessons several afternoons a week. I think that this was a course designed mainly for foreigners. Yet Marilyn felt it was essential for her. "I guess that's what I get for dropping out of school," she would say on her way to the class.

"All I want is to play something different. Like a queen or a great actress or a lady doctor. Anything." Marilyn wanted the challenge of a new kind of role.

Her Cherie in *Bus Stop* was a down-and-out bar girl
who wanted to make it in Hollywood. Cherie was too
close to home for Marilyn. She was too much like her.
Her Elsie in *The Prince and the Showgirl* had more
class, but was still a chorus girl. These were not the
great ladies Marilyn dreamed about playing. "The
Strasbergs say I can," she kept answering herself.
That, to her, would be real acting. That would be the
challenge. She wasn't sure she could do it, but she
wanted very, very much to try.

Mr. Miller's role in Marilyn's efforts to transform
herself into a "serious dramatic actress" was unclear.
Surely, as a playwright, he represented the very top of
serious dramatic art. Marilyn's marriage to him, in
itself, was a symbol of her commitment to kiss Hollywood good-bye. In a sense, Mr. Miller was her protection against ever being used just as a pretty blonde
with a voluptuous body. Yet Mr. Miller did not seem
overly concerned about Marilyn's "dumb blonde"
roles in *Bus Stop* and *Prince*. "Arthur liked them
both," Marilyn scowled. She shifted to her giggle. "I
think Arthur secretly likes dumb blondes. Never had
one before me. Some help he is." No, it didn't appear
that Mr. Miller would lead the fight to have Marilyn
play a great lady. The Strasbergs seemed to be her
major saviors.

I had first assumed that the Strasbergs were helping
Marilyn out of pure friendship, but Marilyn was
forever writing checks to them. "They really need the
money," she would say in a concerned voice. I'm not
sure what the checks were for—Paula's coaching,
donations to the Studio, or what. Whatever, Marilyn
was very lavish with her checkbook. In fact, Marilyn
was extremely generous to everyone, including myself.

As the weather turned cold, Marilyn became very

concerned that my wool coat wasn't heavy enough. One day she saw me sneeze. "That's enough!" she insisted. "I won't let you get sick." She grabbed her checkbook, which was almost always near her bed, and wrote me a check for $300. "Now go right to Bloomingdale's and buy yourself a coat. A warm coat. O.K.?" I refused, but she wouldn't take no for an answer. "You better!" I had never seen her so determined. This was one of her rare orders; I would have insulted her by not taking it.

Marilyn was equally lavish with my salary. I never earned less than $150 a week, which was excellent pay at the time. Often I earned far more, especially when she was unhappy and had me stay late to keep her company. Never once did I mention money to her. She didn't ask either. She just gave.

I assume that May, Hattie, and Cora, the cleaning girl, were also very well treated. For example, Marilyn insisted that a bottle of Chivas Regal be kept on hand for Cora. "Cleaning's hard enough," Marilyn said. "She deserves a big drink."

During our late nights together, Marilyn decided that I, too, deserved a drink. Although she had never before shared her liquor supply with me, she now would appear hurt unless I joined her in some champagne. It didn't take much to make me tipsy, so I never had more than a few sips. As long as Marilyn was sure I was comfortable, she would talk forever. Initially, most of her conversations would concern her "serious dramatic actress" situation. Yet, there always seemed to be deeper, more important problems that she hesitated to go into. She hated Hollywood, but why? "I want to show them," she'd say. "Them" was Hollywood, though I still had no idea exactly what "they" had done to her. I was soon to learn.

4

Early one evening when I was sewing one of Marilyn's dresses in the back bedroom, I started humming to myself. The song was "L'Oro Fugito," the lovely aria from the opera *Tosca*. All Italian children learn these songs and never cease to enjoy them. I guess I must have gotten carried away, for, before long, I was singing the words as if I were Caruso.

"Oh, Lena!" Marilyn exclaimed, standing at the doorway in her usual nakedness.

"I'm sorry," I said, stopping the song. "I hope I didn't wake you up."

"No. No. Oh, keep singing. That's so beautiful," Marilyn said. "I didn't know you could sing."

I was too embarrassed to perform, yet Marilyn kept urging me. "What is it? What does it mean?" she pressed.

I told her that it came from an opera and that it was

the lament of a woman whose lover has drowned himself.

"Opera!" Marilyn said. "Paula [Strasberg] said she'd take me. Maybe we can all go." She looked very excited for a moment, as if something new might come into her life. Then her smile dissolved into a very downcast look. "I'll never go anywhere. Never." She stood there, beginning to cry.

"You can go anywhere," I assured her. "Anywhere in the world."

"Who with?" she asked sadly. "Who with? By myself?"

"Mr. Miller, your friends . . ."

"What friends? I ain't got nobody." She threw herself weeping onto the small bed next to where I was sewing. "Sing to me, Lena, please."

I hummed a little more of the aria, which seemed to calm her down.

"You sound so nice," Marilyn complimented me over and over.

"I wanted to be a singer when I was a little girl," I confessed to her. "But in Italy 'nice girls' weren't supposed to become singers. Mothers, yes. Singers, no."

"Why not?"

I tried to explain why in Italy becoming a singer or an actress wasn't considered respectable. I told Marilyn about my great disappointment when my father wouldn't let me become a singer or even dream about it. My father, as I had told her before, was dead set against my becoming a nun. "He said it was better to be a prostitute than a nun. So I didn't become a nun. Then I got the idea of being a singer, but he didn't like singers either. He was too strict. He thought prostitutes and singers were all the same, so he sent me to seamstress school. I wish I had grown up here. Maybe here I could have sung and been a big success, not just a seamstress. America is better. You can become anything you want." I must have seemed depressed.

"No, you can't. You can't," Marilyn said, with an unusual sense of bitterness in her voice. "Your father was right. Singers, actresses, prostitutes. What's the difference? It's all rotten."

"There's a big difference here," I said. "Why, look at you. You're a big star. You're a big success. Everybody knows you."

Marilyn shook her head. "Prostitute," was all she said. "Prostitute. You had a . . . father . . . to tell you." She started crying again.

I brought her some champagne to revive her spirits. It helped. "Lena, never feel bad that you didn't become a singer. You had a wonderful father. He was right. Look at me."

"Everyone wishes they could be like you," I said.

"No, they don't. They laugh at me. What am I . . . nothing . . . a prostitute."

"Come on," I urged her to cheer up. "Everybody loves you."

She just stared at me, laughing a little between the tears. "It's all so crazy," she said. "Star . . . if I only had someone to talk to . . . a father . . . Lena, I didn't even have a mother."

I came over and sat next to her and held her while she sobbed. "But the lady in the picture." I mentioned the woman by her bed.

"She didn't care. No one did." Marilyn was finally to begin discussing her early childhood. It helped me to understand why she was so miserable, why she felt all alone. "I'll tell you about her, about me," she said, "if you promise not to hate me."

"Why would I?"

"Because I did some bad things. Things that made me hate myself. Things your father kept you from doing."

"I'd never hate you. You know that."

"I want to show you how you become a . . . a star. I don't want you to look back and be sorry you didn't become a singer. You're lucky like you are. Really!"

Marilyn wiped her eyes on the pillowcase. I gave her some Kleenex instead. She sniffled away her tears, then asked me to come back into her room with her. "I feel better . . . safer there," she said. Once she was curled up in her bed, with another split of Piper in her hand and me at her side, she began to reminisce.

"The only thing I really remember is that I was all by myself. All alone. For so long." Marilyn told me that she was the illegitimate daughter of a woman who worked in one of the film studios. "Her name was Gladys Monroe Baker, and my real name was Norma Jean Baker," Marilyn said, as if talking about total strangers. "They changed it when they decided to build me up. They change whatever they want to." The "they," I soon understood, referred to the men who controlled the Hollywood movie studios, the ones who made the decisions about which movies would be made and which people would become "stars."

"I was a mistake," Marilyn said. "My mother didn't want to have me." She told me that sometimes she would pretend that her father was a famous movie star. "I had dreams about Clark Gable being my father." But she admitted that she really didn't know, and that she was never close enough to her mother to find out. "I guess she never wanted me," Marilyn said sadly, describing how her mother had entrusted her as a little baby to a foster family. Mrs. Baker would come to visit Marilyn from time to time, but there seemed to be little, if any, love there. "She paid them to look after me."

The fact that her own mother bought Marilyn's care instead of giving it herself was very painful. Her mother was divorced, but still young, she said. "I probably got in her way. I know I must have disgraced her. A divorced woman has enough problems in getting a man, I guess, but one with an illegitimate baby . . . I wish . . . I still wish . . . she had wanted me."

What surprised me a bit was that no matter how unhappy Marilyn may have been at her mother's absence, it never made her cry. Not having a father was an entirely different matter. The mere mention of the word would cause her to halt, and trying to discuss it always caused her to break down. "Wouldn't he have even wanted to see what I was, how I turned out?" she'd ask painfully. "Didn't he care at all? I kept thinking when I was at these people's homes, these strange homes, I kept thinking, hoping that one day, a nice man would come and say, 'I'm here to take my daughter.' Then I would have been safe. I kept hoping. Sometimes I remember even dressing up in whatever clothes I had, thinking that this was the day he'd come. I wanted to be ready. But he never came. No one ever came." I couldn't fight back my own tears. When Marilyn saw me crying, her own weeping became even more intense. I had to hold her; I couldn't have cared more for my own sister.

That was enough for one night, but Marilyn, over the course of a few weeks, insisted on sharing her whole story with me. She described how she was shuttled from one foster home to another, and how her mother was taken away from her altogether and placed in an asylum. "My mother was in a crazy house, and her mother was in a crazy house. Oh, God, I don't want to end up like that." Although the mother was in a sanitarium, she still was somehow able to pay to keep Marilyn in the foster homes. (Perhaps the state welfare fund paid for this.)

Marilyn had very few happy memories about her childhood. She did remember one elderly English family who let her have sips of liquor with them. For a little girl, this was a great thrill. "That's where I learned to drink," she smiled. "They were pretty nice people, too. They didn't pay much attention to me, but they didn't treat me like a slave, either. They just left me alone most of the time. No one, none of the families, ever seemed to notice me."

What hurt Marilyn especially was that these foster families weren't even substitute families for her, just people who kept her for money, for a certain period. None of the families seemed to want to adopt her. "Nobody ever called me their daughter. No one ever held me. No one kissed me. Nobody. And I was afraid to call anyone 'Mom' or 'Dad.' I knew I didn't have any. They knew, too. What could I say?"

A terrible experience for Marilyn came when she was, as she said, "taken away" to an orphan home. "At least before, I was with people. They may not have wanted me, but it was better than the Home. That was like prison. Besides, I wasn't really an orphan. An orphan doesn't have any parents. All the other kids there had parents that were dead. I had at least one parent. But she didn't want me. I was too ashamed to try to explain it to the other kids there."

The orphanage, like other of her foster homes, was remembered by Marilyn chiefly for the chores she had to do. "Dishes, dishes, dishes. I knew I was going to grow up to be a dishwasher. That's all I ever learned." The Home was apparently not cruel, but very boring. The orphans were all taken to school together, taken back, all assigned their chores in the strict routine, and all were required to bunk together in a dormitory. There was little privacy, though for Marilyn the closeness did not see her make any friends. Because she had never had the opportunity to talk with any relatives, Marilyn said that she was very shy and quiet. "I never felt like I belonged, even at the Home," she said. "The only time I was happy was when they took us to a movie. I loved movies. That was the only fun I ever had. The stars were my friends. That was my freedom."

Eventually, Marilyn was "rescued" from the Home by a woman she called her "Aunt Grace." This wasn't actually her relative but a friend of her mother's from her job at the film studio. Grace was made Marilyn's guardian when Mrs. Baker was in the sanitarium. Marilyn pleaded with Grace to get her out of the orphanage, where she had been for almost two years. She was eleven at the time. Grace took her out, but the foster homes that followed were not much better. In one the family had children of its own, and did absolutely nothing to make Marilyn feel part of the group. "The kids didn't want me. Neither did the parents. When I sat at the table to eat, they all talked to each other, but not to me. I even had to do the dishes all by myself. It was awful."

Aunt Grace eventually got Marilyn out of this home, too, and into others, but things went from bad to worse. Marilyn was starting to develop. She became very self-conscious, particularly of her breasts. Furthermore, she didn't have much knowledge about the "facts of life," other than what she heard in the playground whispers and snickers. Too bashful to discuss things with her Aunt Grace and without a friend to guide her, Marilyn learned the very hardest way. One night one of her "foster fathers" invited her to come and chat with him. The rest of the family was out.

"He had never really talked to me before. It felt good to have someone pay attention to me." Then he gave her some whiskey. It was the first drink she had had since she had been with the English couple years ago. Because she had drunk with the English people, she didn't get suspicious of this unusual hospitality. Then the man started kissing her. "At first it was nice to be held and kissed. No one ever kissed me. But then . . . then he wouldn't stop." Still, Marilyn kept her composure when she described how the foster parent ordered her to take her clothes off. "I thought I had to do what he said. Whatever he said." She was used to taking orders. Then he forced himself on her. "I didn't scream. I didn't do anything. It hurt a lot at first, then I didn't feel anything. I just lay there. I just cried."

Marilyn told Grace that she was very unhappy at this home, but she couldn't tell her why. Grace finally took Marilyn to live with her and her husband, who had several children by an earlier marriage. At last Marilyn was with people who were the closest thing to friends she had ever known. Yet she was torturing herself by concealing her terrible experience. She kept feeling sicker and sicker, both because of her guilt and because of the pains in her body that wouldn't go away. She was pregnant.

Marilyn said that she concealed her secret until it was far too late to have done anything else except have the baby. "I was afraid she'd kill me when I told her," Marilyn said about Grace. "But she didn't get mad at all. She just took me to a doctor. Later on, I went to a hospital, where I had the baby . . . my baby. I was so scared but it was wonderful. It was a little boy. I hugged him and kissed him. I just kept touching him. I couldn't believe this was my baby. I had him in the hospital for a few days. But when it was time for me to leave, the doctor and a nurse came in with Grace. They all looked real strange and said they'd be taking the baby. It was like I was being kicked in the head. I begged them, 'Don't take my baby.' But Grace gave me a dirty look and said it was the best thing. She said I was too young to take care of it, that I had caused enough trouble, and to shut up. So they took my baby from me . . . and I never saw him again.'' Marilyn was sobbing out of control. She grabbed a bottle of sleeping pills by her bed, and popped one in her mouth, washing it down with champagne. Marilyn must have used up an entire box of Kleenex that night. She just threw the wet tissues all over the bed and on the floor. She didn't care. I didn't blame her.

When the pill began to take effect and she quieted down a bit, Marilyn insisted on talking some more about her baby. ''See, Lena, I can have a baby,'' she boasted, referring to the difficulties she had had in recent years in trying to have a child with Mr. Miller. ''I did it once. I'll do it again. I will.''

I couldn't keep myself from asking her if she knew what had happened to her first baby.

''I don't know,'' she answered sadly. ''I was afraid to ask. I thought they would send me back to the home. Oh, Lena, those days in the hospital nursing my baby were the happiest days I ever spent. I hope he's all right, hope he has a nice family. Maybe Grace was right. What kind of mother could I have been then? I was just a kid.'' She started crying again. ''I wish I could see him.''

''Why not?'' I asked. ''Can't you find out what happened to him?''

''Oh, no,'' she said. ''I couldn't do that to him. I hope he's happy. He has his own life. I don't want to spoil it for him. At first, when they took him, I wanted to run away and go and take him and just live together, me and my baby. But I didn't have any money or anything, and I was frightened. So I gave up. I just gave up." As Marilyn slowly drifted off to sleep, I covered her up with the sheets and a blanket. I sat with her for another half hour to make sure she was fast asleep, before I went home. As I strolled home through the dark, empty streets of the East Side, I thought to myself how lucky I was. I had a family to go home to, two wonderful little boys. Poor Marilyn. What did she have?

The next day, Marilyn wanted to resume her story. She loved having someone to talk to, and she evidently could sense I cared. Though there wasn't much I could do to change things for her, I was happy to be a good listener. After she lost her baby, she told me, her Aunt Grace decided that Marilyn would be better off married. Grace's family, she explained, was going to move. Marilyn was faced with three possibilities: find another family, go back to the orphanage, or get married. After all, she was fifteen and almost full-grown. She had had a child. Wasn't it a little strange for her to go back to an orphanage? Maybe marriage wouldn't be all that bad. "I was so mixed up at that point. I did what I was told," Marilyn said. "I couldn't think. I just didn't want to go back to the Home. Never! I only wish a husband had been around earlier. Then I could have kept my baby."

"I don't think they [Grace's family] trusted me at all," Marilyn said. She described how she had continued to fill out ("I was pretty well built"), and that all the boys at the high school had started noticing her. "All of a sudden I became popular. Before, no one would even look at me, much less talk. Now all the guys were saying 'Hello' and flirting like crazy. I had learned to put on makeup. Wow! It really made a difference." The biggest difference was that Grace and her family were deathly afraid Marilyn would become pregnant again. Grace had complained bitterly to Marilyn about the expense of the hospital and constantly chastised her about "being careful" whenever she was around boys.

One boy Grace could trust was Jim Dougherty, literally the boy next door. ("I could never spell his name," Marilyn said.) "Jim," Marilyn said, "was handsome, well-mannered, and had a good job—and a car. What I couldn't figure out was what a guy like Jim would want with me." Marilyn was always unsure of herself, even when she was reaching her first bloom as a young beauty. She talked about being "built," never about being pretty.

Nevertheless, once the proposition had been made by Grace, Jim did seem to want Marilyn, and a great deal at that. "You see, we went to this dance together," Marilyn reminisced. "Grace had to beg his mother to make him take me. I was fifteen, he was nineteen and already had lots of girlfriends his age. I kind of looked up to him at the time, you know, especially because he had that car. He had been a big shot at the high school, too. I was at the same one, and was a nobody. I even asked a girl I knew to pretend she was a boy and dance with me. I wanted to be sure I knew how, so I wouldn't step on his feet. Well, as soon as we got to the dance and they started playing those slow numbers, the close ones, he didn't seem to mind at all. It was even funny that he was the one who stepped on my feet. I think he was pretty excited." Marilyn began to giggle.

It wasn't the kind of romance she had seen in the movies, Marilyn admitted, "but it was nice being liked by someone. He did like me a lot." Grace apparently kept the pressure up on Jim's mother, and the couple were married in 1942, in the middle of World War II. "He wasn't my choice," Marilyn explained. "But I had never had a choice. Grace didn't give me any choice. She was leaving town, and maybe she wanted to make sure I would be taken care of. Once I tried to tell her I wasn't in love, and she just snickered, 'What do you know about love? You'll be in love after you get married. Just do what I say.' So I did. But I never fell in love."

Marilyn didn't say much about the marriage, other than she tried to become a good housewife. "I was good with the dishes," she smiled. "I had enough practice. But I never really learned to cook."

"Cooking's easy," I said.

"For you. I'm sure glad you're here. I can't even warm things up without burning them."

Marilyn had dropped out of high school, though that hadn't seemed to bother her. "I wasn't much in high school. I wasn't much anywhere. So I figured a housewife was as good as I could hope to be."

"What about becoming a movie star?"

Marilyn laughed loudly. "You kidding? Me? That never even crossed my mind then. I was lucky just to go and see a movie. Be in them, ha! And now, here I am, in them. Funny."

"So when did you decide?"

"I didn't decide. That's the crazy part. I'll tell you."

Marilyn said that although she wanted a child desperately, she had hesitated, both because of the uncertainties of the war (Jim might have had to go any time) and because she wasn't sure that this marriage, which Grace had pressured her into, would last forever. "I was really beginning to like him more and more," Marilyn said. "He was the first person who ever liked me that much and that was nice. But then he had to go overseas."

Before Jim shipped out, he and Marilyn lived on a base on an island near Los Angeles. Aside from wives, there weren't many women on the base. Marilyn, who had developed even more by then, definitely enjoyed the attention she got, particularly when she wore a bathing suit to the beach on Saturday. "In high school, the guys had started to notice me, but out on Catalina it was incredible. It was like . . . like I was a movie star. I never had thought I was all that great, but, gee, with all these guys staring and grinning . . . I like being told how nice I looked. I liked it a lot. All my life I was ignored, and now I started looking at myself for a long time in the mirror just to see what was so great. At first Jim was proud, then he got worried. He didn't trust me . . . and I guess he was right."

When Jim was away, Marilyn went to live with his parents back in Los Angeles. Marilyn described her existence there as so dull that she started going out to bars by herself in the afternoon to drink alone. "That helped kill time. I didn't have anything to look forward to. I liked drinking." She said that she would go from one bar to another. She made her rounds in Jim's car. One bar was rather unusual. There were a lot of single girls there, and a lot of men. The women all seemed to leave with the guys after a drink or two. She had never seen such a friendly place. Men had tried to pick Marilyn up before, she said, but she had always refused on the grounds that she was a married woman. "It was fun, when they tried to pick me up," Marilyn confessed. "Most of them weren't so hot, though. All the good men seemed to be off fighting somewhere."

Yet at this last bar, there were other compensations. One person, a middle-aged man who told her he worked in the film business, just wouldn't give up. He offered Marilyn fifteen dollars to leave with him. "At first I was shocked. I hadn't been around enough to know what was going on. He had a suit on, so I didn't think he could hurt me. When I started thinking about a new dress I wanted and couldn't afford, well . . . I was pretty drunk, too . . . so I said O.K. I still wasn't sure what he wanted to do." Marilyn described how they left the bar for the hotel where the man was staying. He asked her to take off her clothes. "I thought that was a pretty good deal for fifteen dollars. At the beach I was almost naked . . . for nothing."

However, there was more to the bargain. When the man started taking his suit off, she said she shrieked. Then he explained to her what he wanted to do. At first, she said, she wanted to run. "But then I thought about it. I didn't really love Jim, but I let him do what he wanted. It didn't bother me that much. So what was the difference?" Marilyn did tell the man that he had to wear some protection, like Jim did. She certainly didn't want to take the risk of getting pregnant. "He was pretty annoyed. He had to put all his clothes back on and go down and find a drugstore," Marilyn grinned. "He got back real fast."

According to Marilyn, she went back to this bar and others like it fairly often. For her, it was an easy way to pick up extra money. Further, she said she got a kick out of seeing how excited the men would get when she took her clothes off. "They would tell me that I was beautiful, wonderful, you name it. They all acted the same way." It made her feel that she had a special power over men. "I didn't have to say a word. Just take my dress off." She shook her head in disbelief and smiled. She said that the men didn't notice that she herself wasn't getting all aroused by what they were doing. "They just took their own pleasure and ran. I didn't care," she said. "I was used to it. I didn't expect anything."

One of the men she met this way told her he was a Hollywood agent. "These bars were full of agents," Marilyn said. "Or at least guys who claimed they were. A lot of the girls who hung out there hoped they would break into movies that way." This agent was nicer than most, she said. "He really liked me, I think. We met a few times. He told me that I was special, and that I had the looks to be in movies. He said that if I did *this*, what I was doing, with the right men, I might be able to be in pictures. I laughed at him and told him I couldn't act. And he said neither can so-and-so or so-and-so. He named some of the big actresses then. I thought about it after he left. You know, I decided, maybe he was right." Then and there, Marilyn started thinking about becoming a movie star. "At first, it was just a thought. But it got bigger and bigger. It became my ambition, my only ambition, the first one I ever had."

Marilyn told me how she began paying increasing attention to her appearance, buying dresses that flattered her figure, wearing more makeup, fixing her hair. "These men gave me something to live for." However, she said that her secret afternoons were making her very nervous. What if Jim came home and discovered her? What if she ran into one of his friends on leave? She became so afraid of being caught, she said, that she got Jim's mother to get her a job at the defense plant where Mrs. Dougherty worked. The job did not last long. Marilyn soon got up the courage to join a modeling agency, and quickly got a great many assignments. "There was still a lot of sex. The guys sort of expected it as part of the job. But now instead of paying me, they'd take my picture. And I liked that better. I loved to pose. I was amazed how the pictures usually made me look better than I was in real life."

To protect her increasing independence, Marilyn said that she moved away from the Doughertys and in with the elderly aunt of Aunt Grace, Ana Lower, or "Aunt Ana," as Marilyn would call her fondly. After Jim came home on a brief leave, Marilyn decided that she had to have a divorce. "I didn't feel any different with him than I did with strangers," she admitted. She felt that she needed to be free, and also that the marriage wasn't fair to Jim, either. "He deserved a wife who loved him. He was a good person. He didn't deserve me." That was the only time I saw Marilyn cry about Jim. Generally, she was rather cold in discussing him, but leaving him, the one man who had shown true affection for her, was a drastic step for her to take. "I still feel bad about it," she whispered to me.

With Jim out of her life, Marilyn could pursue her Hollywood dream without any distractions. Most "models" in Los Angeles wanted to get into movies, she said, and her agency had certain contacts at the different studios. Because her picture began to appear in a number of magazines, she was able to get a screen test at Twentieth Century-Fox. "I couldn't believe it was happening to me," Marilyn smiled, still seeming amazed, even as a star, that she had gotten the break. Passing the test with flying colors, Marilyn got a contract. It was only for $75 a week. Other girls also won similar contracts, but most of them got nowhere. Yet it was a start. Marilyn had her foot in the door.

"What did you do in your screen test?" I asked. "What part did you play?"

She just laughed. "Part? I didn't say a word. Blonde hair and breasts, that's how I got started."

Suddenly, she got on her knees on the bed and looked at her chest in the mirror. She held up her breasts. "They were better then, firmer," she moaned, and drank some more champagne. Then she ran her fingers through her hair, greasy from days of neglect. She made another face, as if she were not at all happy with the way she looked now. Marilyn said that for her test she had dyed her hair a brighter shade of blonde. "The blonder the better. Men have this weakness for blonde hair. It's true! I told you, Lena, your father was right. Singers, actresses, prostitutes, the same. They all get started the same way. At least I did." Her face turned very serious. "What do you think, Lena? Was I wrong? Maybe I just should have been a housewife? What do you think?"

"If you weren't good, you wouldn't have become a star," I reminded her. "If that's what you wanted to be, then it was right for you."

"No, no. Not so," Marilyn sighed. "I couldn't act. All I had was my blonde hair and a body men liked. The reason I got ahead is that I was lucky and met the right men." Marilyn told me that the best thing that happened to her at Twentieth Century-Fox was meeting a man named Joe Schenck, who was one of the founders of the company. She told me how all the top bosses would make it a point to "inspect" all the new starlets who had come on the lot. "The worst thing a girl could do was to say no to these guys. She'd be finished," Marilyn said.

Marilyn described how all the starlets would put themselves on "review" at special parties given at two big nightclubs. These private affairs were usually given the night before the opening of a major singer or other name act. "Everybody in Hollywood was there to check over the new girls," Marilyn said. "We had our choice. We could be picked up by some handsome young actor and have a little fun. Or we could go off with some old bigwig and make a few dollars, or, if we were really lucky, we could get him to help us find a part. Most of us always tried to find an old guy. I got to be known pretty quick. They considered me a 'hot number' back then," she laughed.

To give me more of an idea of what Hollywood life was like, Marilyn told me all about Mr. Schenck. He was a bald, bearlike man of about seventy, with a huge nose and a huge cigar. A Russian immigrant, Mr. Schenck really succeeded all on his own. He had begun in the drugstore business in New York. He told Marilyn he worked on the Bowery. Irving Berlin was a singing waiter in a restaurant next door to the pharmacy where Mr. Schenck learned to fill prescriptions. Next Mr. Schenck went into the amusement park business. He had owned Palisades Park, which lit up the New Jersey side of the Hudson River across from Manhattan. It was a place where Marilyn had mentioned wanting to go on several occasions. She thought it would be fun to go on all the rides. Soon Schenck branched out from roller coasters to motion pictures. He had been married to silent movie star Norma Talmadge, who left Schenck for George Jessel. He had later been engaged to British beauty Merle Oberon, and linked with many other Hollywood sirens. He had a million-dollar yacht. Mr. Schenck had a reputation around Hollywood as a man who could, and did, buy any woman he wanted. Now he wanted Marilyn, whose name had been changed when she signed on at Fox.

"He had me come over to his house," she said. "It was a mansion. I had never been any place like that. He had the greatest food, too. That's when I learned about champagne. What I liked was hearing about all the stars I had seen in the movies. Joe knew them all.

He seemed to have this thing about breasts. After
dinner, he told me to take my clothes off and he would
tell me Hollywood stories. I would just listen to these
wonderful tales about John Barrymore, Charlie Chap-
lin, Valentino, everybody, and Mr. Schenck would
play with my breasts. What could I say? He didn't
want to do much else, since he was getting old, but
sometimes he asked me to kiss him—down there."
Marilyn grimaced, pointing to her privates. "I never
want to have to do that anymore," Marilyn blurted
out, with what seemed to be intense, pent-up disgust.
"It would seem like hours, and nothing would happen,
but I was afraid to stop. I felt like gagging, but if I did, I
thought he'd get insulted. Sometimes, he'd just fall
asleep. If he stayed awake, he'd pat my head, like a
puppy, and thank me. All the other girls thought I
really had it made. Ha! I kept going back. At least the
food was good."

All Marilyn's efforts for Mr. Schenck seemed to
have been in vain. She was dropped from her contract
after her first year. Despite Mr. Schenck's former
power, he had recently gone to prison in a case of labor
racketeering in the film business. Even though he had
been pardoned, the cloud of gangland connections still
hung over his head. He was thus unable to throw his
full weight around to "make Marilyn a star" over-
night. "I kept thinking all he had to do was make one
call for me but he wouldn't push. 'It'll happen,' was all
he said." Still he kept having her drop by for story-
telling sessions and told her to be patient. "I didn't have
anywhere else to go. I didn't have a job. Joe was my
only hope."

Her hoping eventually paid off. After several frustrating months of unemployment, supporting herself
by modeling and barhopping, Marilyn was introduced
by Joe to Harry Cohn, the head of Columbia Pictures.

"Joe [Schenck] was like Clark Gable by comparison. Mr. Cohn wasn't even the kind who said hello first. He just told you to get in bed. For him, women were slaves." Whatever, Cohn put Marilyn's name up in lights, with second billing in a movie called *Ladies of the Chorus*. "I kept driving past the theater with my name on the marquee. Marilyn Monroe! Wow! Was I excited! I wished they were using Norma Jean so that all the kids at the home and schools who never noticed me could see it! They'd have been surprised." The movie was far from a hit, but Marilyn got to sing and dance. She played a burlesque dancer who met a rich man. The man falls in love with Marilyn without knowing her identity. Although he finds out anyway, love conquers all. Marilyn frequently talked about that ending. She liked it.

The only sad ending was that Cohn and Columbia dropped Marilyn after this picture. After more anxious waiting, Marilyn told me how she got a bit part in the Marx Brothers movie *Love Happy*. "No acting, just sex again. I had to wiggle across a room. I practiced jiggling my backside for a week. Groucho loved it. His eyes popped out. I remember he made this joke off-screen. He said, 'Young lady, I think you're a case of arrested development. With your development, somebody's bound to get arrested.' That helped me a lot to relax. Groucho's great!"

Despite this spotty progress, Marilyn was beginning to panic. Joe Schenck clearly wasn't going to demand the kind of favors for her his status entitled him to. She needed a new sponsor who would give her the crucial push. Not that she was idle. Marilyn said that she was taking acting lessons. "I wanted to learn something. Maybe then I wouldn't be so scared." Again, just as at the home, Marilyn felt that she didn't "belong" in pictures. Yet she wanted to belong. She

simply needed some encouragement, and got it from
Johnny Hyde, who, she proudly said, was the most
important agent in Hollywood. Mr. Schenck may have
been resting on his laurels but Mr. Hyde was anything
but inactive. Agents evidently have hundreds of sets of
eyes, always on the lookout. Once Hyde spotted
Marilyn in *Love Happy* he was so taken with her that
he wanted to manage her career.

Hyde had originally worked booking acts for one of
Joe Schenck's theater chains, and had done so well
that he became a Schenck protégé. Hyde went on to
represent a great many stars, including Mickey
Rooney, Amos and Andy, Mae West, Lana Turner,
Bob Hope, Rita Hayworth. Marilyn felt that Schenck
had put in a good word for her to Hyde, though she
didn't seem to really need it. "He told me he had
discovered Lana Turner, and now he was discovering
me, and that I'd go even further. That made me
dizzy."

Nonetheless, again sex entered the picture. Hyde
fell in love even more with Marilyn the woman than
with Marilyn the actress. "He was so sweet," Marilyn
said, "but I just couldn't get excited about him as a
man. You know, I had all these ideas about tall, dark
and handsome, and all that. He wasn't." Hyde was
dapper and well-dressed but tiny, only five feet tall.
"He had the best clothes in town," Marilyn said, "but
they were like doll's clothes." Marilyn described him
as being obsessed with his masculinity. When they
made love, he'd get upset if she didn't put on a display
of ecstasy. "I didn't mind doing it," Marilyn shrugged.
"But nothing seemed to excite me. It wasn't him. It
was me. But he took it personally, and I had to act
like it was the thrill of my life. I wish it had been.
Johnny was good, really good, to me. He even wanted
to get married. But after Jim [Dougherty] I just didn't

want to get married unless I was head over heels in love. This wasn't it."

Love or not, Johnny Hyde did everything for Marilyn. He took her to all the big restaurants and parties. Just being seen with him, even though she towered over him, made all the right people want to know about her. "I loved going out to all those restaurants with Johnny. I wish Arthur would go out more often," Marilyn said in a disappointed tone. "At first I was kind of embarrassed 'cause Johnny was so short, but everyone looked up to him, all the stars."

More valuable than being seen, Johnny Hyde got Marilyn her two most important roles to date, *The Asphalt Jungle,* a realistic crime melodrama, and *All About Eve,* a sophisticated comedy about the theater. They were small roles, Marilyn playing a kept woman, in one to a crooked lawyer, in the other to a vicious drama critic. "I started as a dumb blonde whore. I'll end as one," she complained to me. Yet Marilyn admitted that she couldn't complain about all the excellent exposure these two huge hits provided her. "They and the calendar, that did it for me," Marilyn said.

The calendar she referred to was some nude camera work she had done to support herself when she was out of work several years earlier. "Getting paid to take my clothes off was the easiest thing in the world. I mean, I never seem to have them on anyway." Marilyn giggled, staring at her naked body in the mirror. "How did I ever get so fat? You should have seen me then. Oh, Lena, don't let me eat so much." She never stopped thinking of her appearance.

America might have criticized another actress for posing in the nude, but when it was made public that the beautiful blonde on the calendar was Marilyn, nobody cared. Everybody wanted a copy. She became one of America's favorite pinups. "The studio put out all this stuff about the orphan home and all, so everyone felt sorry for me. They thought it was the best publicity I could get. It really worked."

Unfortunately, Marilyn had lost her best friend in Hollywood, Johnny Hyde, to a heart attack. He was only in his fifties. She cried when she spoke about him. "Oh, God, if I had married him maybe he would have lived. He used to say that I was the only one who could save his life, but I thought he was joking. Then he died, he just died. And then I decided I did love him, but it was too late. I hated myself. Jesus, so he wasn't a dreamboat. He was my friend. He cared. He loved me. What are looks? I could have saved him. I killed him, I killed him!" Marilyn started screaming and tearing her hair out, which she did whenever she got extremely upset. Her feeling that she caused someone's death would surface again several years later when Clark Gable died of a heart attack after making *The Misfits* with her.

I told her that Mr. Hyde's time had simply come, that it wasn't her fault, and that having her with him made his last years happier. I did my best to be positive, yet it didn't help that much. "He was happy with me," she said. "But he would have been even happier if I had married him."

"You can't read the future," I replied.

"Yeah, but I had this sense, this feeling that I should have said yes. I was being spoiled. Who was I? I never had anything and suddenly I want everything to be perfect. He was the kindest person in the business. By far."

Before his death, Hyde had gotten Marilyn another contract with Twentieth Century-Fox at a much higher salary, over $500 a week. Still, without him around to convince the studio bosses to develop her as an actress, Marilyn was stuck with the dumb blonde image. The man she blamed most for keeping her trapped was Darryl F. Zanuck, the head of the company. According to Marilyn, Zanuck felt she was a dumb blonde, and nothing more, that Americans liked dumb blondes, and that his duty as a businessman was to give the public exactly what it wanted. "His idea was that no one would pay their money for a ticket to see me in a decent role." Marilyn said that Zanuck ignored her completely. Whether she tried to act seductive or sweet around him, nothing seemed to work. "I would have been happy to do anything—you know," she winked, "to get him to let me try something different. He wasn't interested at all. Every other guy was. Why wasn't he?" she wondered.

At first, Marilyn said, she respected Mr. Zanuck's judgment. After all, he was the boss, and if she was getting paid to be a dumb blonde, she should cash her check and be grateful. On the other hand, drama coaches and other actors and actresses she met told her she could be more, that she had talent. "So many people told me that I started believing them." There was also constant complaining among the actors of how the business people and the artistic people were always at odds. Soon the bitter gossip started to affect Marilyn. Maybe she was being exploited, she began thinking. Whatever, at the box office, things for Marilyn were better than ever. She was becoming a big star, no matter how bad the movies were. She might as well have been Miss America. With her 1952 romance with the legendary Joe DiMaggio, her fame was guaranteed. No man in the country could have boosted her public image more than the Baseball King. She became the hottest of hot items.

Of all her early movies, *Gentlemen Prefer Blondes* was by far the one she liked best. It was also a tremendous success. Since I hadn't seen it, Marilyn did her big number, "Diamonds Are a Girl's Best Friend," in her bedroom, using her bed for a stage. She loved to perform, even for an audience of one, kicking and strutting, wearing one of her mink jackets for the scene. "My gold digger routine," she joked. Her favorite line was about "rocks" not losing their shape. I applauded loudly for her, shouting, "Bravo" many times. She loved it, and was truly happy for once. I asked her many times for encores, especially when she was feeling down, and she always agreed. In return, she made me sing her Italian songs like "O Solo Mio" and "Funiculi, Funicula." She was quick to learn the words and join in, even though she had no idea what they meant. Sometimes we sang so loudly in the evenings I thought the neighbors would complain, or at least Mr. Miller, but we never got into any trouble. Nothing seemed to budge him from his study.

"You're pretty good for a dumb blonde," I teased her. It made me feel so good to see her laugh.

Marilyn, then, had told me at least the outlines of her rise to stardom. It was a sad story, and as she promised, it made me feel far less disappointed about never becoming a singer. I would have never wanted to go through what she did to make it in show business.

She clearly wanted to put the past behind her. She loved the idea of being a star, but she hated not only the way she had to use sex to climb the Hollywood ladder but also the way sex dominated her life. If her stardom depended on her willingness to be a sex symbol, she clearly wasn't sure whether that price might not be too high. Marilyn was beautiful. She could be as attractive as any woman. Men of every sort worshiped her. But she didn't want to be lusted for. She wanted respect, something from her earliest days she had never known. She had used sex to break through the studio barriers, but once in, she wanted to act, to be someone. That's why she had come to New York, for a fresh start, with people who appreciated her potential. "The funny thing, Lena," she would say softly, "was that I never knew what I wanted to be. At first, being a star seemed great. But then all my friends . . . well, you know . . . the people who wanted to help me said, 'Don't be a sex star, be an actress. You can.' So I'm here trying. But maybe Zanuck was right. Maybe all this acting is crazy. Maybe I should stay with sex."

Making it as a serious actress would wipe the slate clean; it would pardon her for all the sex that went before. Marilyn groaned. Living up to an image others have set for you is always extremely difficult, and when these "others" are experts like the Strasbergs, the challenge is truly frightening.

One thing was clear. Whatever career moves Marilyn would make, she had no regrets to be out of Hollywood. Los Angeles held few happy memories for her. It was her birthplace but there was nothing there she could call home, family, friends. And even in the film industry, even when her success was mounting, Marilyn still felt as out of place as she did in any foster home. She was never accepted in the star community, and it hurt.

One of the unkindest cuts came from Joan Crawford, who, Marilyn said, was her favorite actress. (Her favorite actor was Tyrone Power, her favorite movie, *Blood and Sand,* with Power cast as a matador.) But Joan Crawford, who could play anything, was Marilyn's idea of success, of "class." When Marilyn won an award from *Photoplay,* the fan magazine, as the top young star of 1953, she went to the dinner to receive her award wearing a tight, sexy gold lamé dress of the sort the studio wardrobe people felt was "perfect" for her. Alas, Joan Crawford thought Marilyn was anything but perfect. Marilyn said she knew something was wrong when she met Miss Crawford in the ladies' room and attempted to tell her how much she admired her. Miss Crawford whisked straight by her, very arrogantly pretending not to have seen Marilyn.

The next day, Joan Crawford exploded to the Hollywood press, attacking Marilyn as a sexual monster, a menace to "family" entertainment, and as Marilyn rephrased it, "a sleazy whore." "I went to pieces. I didn't know about fashion; I relied on people who were supposed to be experts. Experts for the studio. I dressed by the rules—studio rules—and what did I get? Humiliation." Once Joan Crawford, who was at the top of the Hollywood Establishment, had spoken, Marilyn felt she was cursed as a tawdry sexpot, and a laughable one to boot. "I couldn't face anyone," she said. Sex that had helped her was now haunting her. "It was driving me crazy. I had to get out of there. I was sick of being some kind of a freak all my life." Thus when Milton Greene offered Marilyn a fresh start in New York, it was the perfect offer for her. Unfortunately, New York, whether with the Greenes, the Strasbergs, or with Arthur Miller, wasn't working out either. Indeed, it was driving her crazy.

5

"Arthur. It was Arthur. He was why I stayed in New York. He was going to make my life different, better, a lot better," Marilyn would often cry in despair. Evidently the "better" hadn't happened, and she was very frustrated over it. Frequently she told me that Mr. Miller was the key to the existence she wanted to have.

Mr. Miller, Marilyn said, represented many things to her. He was the "nice man," the mystery father, who she dreamed would rescue her from the foster homes. He was Abraham Lincoln, her historical hero; Mr. Miller certainly looked like him. He was smart and sensitive, a great reader and a famous writer. "Arthur was the only 'brain' who liked me for me," Marilyn said with a great deal of pride. "He wasn't just after something. Those other famous guys out in Hollywood, the ones who were supposed to be smart, well, they'd act real nice . . . at first, and then they'd try to

do something. They all had one thing on their minds.
But not Arthur. He cared. He saw what Hollywood
was doing to me. He wouldn't let it happen. He
promised. If I was nothing but a dumb blonde, he
wouldn't have married me . . . would he?'' she asked.
Now she wasn't sure.

The parts the Hollywood producers were sending
Marilyn to consider were still the same old ones—sexy
women, sexy roles. Things hadn't changed. ''Can't he
do anything for me?'' she cried. ''Can't they respect
me the way they respect him?'' Yet, even more important than Mr. Miller's helping her gain her goal as a
serious actress, Marilyn wanted him to be the father of
her children. ''Think how great the kids'll be, Lena.
Think how smart,'' she beamed. Then immediately
doubt set in. ''Lena, do you think I can? Do you? I
want to have a baby. I've got to.''

I wasn't sure which mattered more to her—a family
or a career. ''When you have kids,'' I once asked her,
''what will you do about acting?''

She smiled broadly. ''Nothing! If I have kids—a
kid—that'll be my life. Maybe later, in a long time,
when she grows up, then maybe I might act.'' The
''she'' referred to Marilyn's intense wish to have a girl.
''I want her to have love, happiness, a family—
everything I didn't have. I'll make her the happiest
little girl in the world.''

Soon after they were married in 1956, Marilyn did
become pregnant. Unfortunately, this was unsuc-
cessful after the sixth week. ''I can do it, I know I
can,'' Marilyn said, referring back to the baby she did
have, and who was taken from her. ''I've got to have
my child.'' Then she broke down again. ''It's not fair.
Not fair. I've tried and tried . . . I'm so sick. Can't I
have a baby?'' I did my best to reassure her.

Also, thinking about becoming a mother served to

MARILYN

Marilyn with Johnny Hyde, the top Hollywood agent who got Marilyn her attention-getting roles in *The Asphalt Jungle* and *All About Eve.*

"He was so sweet, but I just couldn't get excited about him as a man. You know, I had all these ideas about tall, dark, and handsome...He wasn't."

The Lester Glassner Collection

One of the many cheesecake shots required of Marilyn by the studios when she was just breaking into Hollywood around 1950.

"I loved to pose."

UPI

Wide World Photos

Joseph Schenck, founder of 20th Century-Fox and film tycoon who taught Marilyn about the movie business.

"The worst thing a girl could do was to say 'no'...Joe was my only hope."

One of Marilyn's earlier films was *Love Happy* with the Marx Brothers.

"No acting, just sex again. I had to wiggle across a room. I practiced jiggling my backside for a week. Groucho loved it."

The Lester Glassner Collection

Marilyn, posing by a bill-
board, is thrilled that she
has finally become a star.

"I kept driving past the
theater with my name on
the marquee. Marilyn
Monroe! Was I excited! I
wished they were using Norma Jean so that all the kids
at the Home and schools
who never noticed me could
see it."

Globe Photos/Bruno Bernard

Joe DiMaggio and Marilyn returning from their
1954 honeymoon in the Orient.

"Joe and I had this crazy thing..."

UPI

Marilyn mesmerizes the troops in Korea during her first and only goodwill tour in 1954.

"I couldn't believe it. There were thousands of them screaming for me. I was scared, but I'd do it again."

Natasha Lytess, Marilyn's first drama coach.

"She was a great teacher, but got really jealous about the men I saw. She thought she was my husband."

J. R. Eyerman, Life Magazine, © 1948, Time, Inc.

The Actors Studio drew Marilyn to New York City in an attempt to escape the "dumb blonde" stereotype Hollywood had forced upon her.

"All I want is to play something different...the Strasbergs say I can."

Popperfoto

UPI

Famous drama coaches and founders of Actors Studio, Lee and Paula Strasberg, were Marilyn's closest friends in New York City.

"They'll never let me down...not for anything."

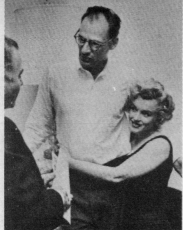

The world was stunned when Marilyn Monroe married Arthur Miller in 1956. People wondered what they could have in common.

"He was going to make my life different...better, a lot better. If I were nothing but a dumb blonde, he wouldn't have married me."

Marilyn and Arthur at a film premiere. One of their rare "on the town" nights.

"I can't go anywhere. I'm a prisoner in this house."

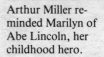

Arthur Miller reminded Marilyn of Abe Lincoln, her childhood hero.

"If Mr. Miller had a beard, he'd look like Lincoln."

With Marilyn is Milton Greene (left), famous fashion photographer, as she received the key to Warner Bros. from Jack Warner. Milton was co-founder of Marilyn Monroe Productions, Inc.

"He told me I'd never be a dumb blonde again."

Marilyn in London for *The Prince and the Showgirl.* With Marilyn and Arthur are her co-star, the great Sir Laurence Olivier, and his beautiful wife, Vivien Leigh.

"Here I was with the most famous actor in the whole world."

A happy pose with Sir Laurence?

"He gave me the dirtiest looks, even when he was smiling."

An early photo of Marilyn the starlet, who loved to eat. Later in her career, when Marilyn didn't like her role as Sugar Kane in *Some Like It Hot,* only eating could cure her depression.

"I'm going to get so fat, they won't let me be in this awful picture."

Globe Photos/Nate Cutler

With *Some Like It Hot* co-star Tony Curtis, director Billy Wilder. Marilyn was upset by Tony's comment that "Kissing her was like kissing Hitler."

Globe Photos

On the set of *Some Like It Hot* in 1958 with Billy Wilder and Paula Strasberg (partially hidden behind MM).

"He's not a director, he's a dictator."

UPI

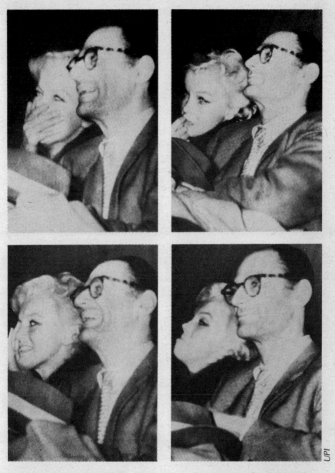

UPI

At an early screening of *Some Like It Hot*. In these rare photos, taken with infrared film, Marilyn shows mixed reactions to her performance, which would become the most famous of her career.

"Did you see how fat I was? Like a pig...Wasn't that movie terrible?"

Marilyn's next movie, *Let's Make Love,* won headlines because of her offscreen romance with Yves Montand. Here she is with Yves and Arthur Miller.

"I love his voice, he's so sexy. Wow!"

The Millers and Montands (Yves and Simone Signoret) had adjoining bungalows at the Beverly Hills Hotel. Marilyn was jealous of Simone, shown here with MM.

"She's not pretty. And she's older than he is. What did she do to get him?"

Marilyn signing an autograph for a young fan at Reno Airport en route to filming Arthur Miller's *The Misfits*. They would break up after this film.

"He could have written me anything, and he comes up with this. If that's what he thinks of me, well, then I'm not for him and he's not for me."

With *Misfits* director John Huston, who also directed her in her breakthrough movie *The Asphalt Jungle,* in which she played a prostitute.

"He treats me like an idiot. 'Honey, this' and 'honey, that.'"

A tender offscreen moment with Clark Gable, whom Marilyn adored.

"He never got angry with me once for blowing a line or being late or anything...he was a gentleman. The best."

Magnum Photos

Magnum Photos/Dennis Stock

The *Misfits* was her most difficult and demanding movie both on and off the set. Here she takes some time off to calm her nerves.

"It's torture. I don't know how long I can stand it. I wish I was home."

Wide World Photos

Eating pasta with her best friend in Hollywood, Montgomery Clift. She was brokenhearted because of Monty's disfigurement in a tragic auto wreck.

"He needs me. He needs someone, I'd love to help him. Oh, but he's so impossible."

Marilyn had a long relationship with Frank Sinatra and had fantasies of marrying him. In fact, she liked him more than she disliked arch rival Elizabeth Taylor. They even sat together at this 1961 Sinatra opening in Las Vegas.

"I can't tie him down, not Frankie, but I'll always love him."

Marilyn with Mexican screenwriter Jose Bolanos, her last (and secret) lover.

"I hear he makes some of the worst movies in Mexico...But what do I care? Everything else he does is incredible."

Joe DiMaggio would always be by her side, even at death in 1962. Here are Joe and son, Joe, Jr., at the funeral in Westwood, California.

"Thank God for Joe, thank God."

distract her from thinking about how hard it was to become a "serious dramatic actress." One time, she was trying, unsuccessfully, to practice or learn some part the Strasbergs had assigned her. "Shit!" I heard her scream, with glass shattering. She had hurled a little champagne bottle across the room, and it had broken into many pieces. Rather than apologize, Marilyn immediately ignored the whole episode. "Hey, Lena, what color do you think we should paint your room when the baby comes? . . . Oh, I hope it comes." Consequently, we got into a long discussion of paint shades and baby furniture. She seemed overjoyed to leave the script in disarray on her bed, and the shattered glass on the rug.

For the father of the child Marilyn wanted so desperately, Mr. Miller seemed a very distant husband. Marilyn maintained the greatest respect for him and his work. She always warned Hattie or Cora to "Hush" if they were chatting too loudly near Mr. Miller's study. If there were ever any guests—agents, lawyers, and the like—she always brought them into her bedroom to entertain them. "Arthur's writing," she'd whisper solemnly. "He needs total quiet."

As for Marilyn and Arthur themselves, their only real contact seemed to occur late at night, after I left. Whenever they ate together, there was little discussion, only longing looks on Marilyn's part. "I wish he'd say more to me," she once confided. "He makes me think I'm stupid. I'm afraid to bring things up, because maybe I am stupid. Gee, he almost scares me sometimes."

On occasion, when Mr. Miller's parents or his friends the Rostens would come for dinner, they would frequently converse in Yiddish. I don't think this was done to hide anything from Marilyn. Yiddish may simply have been an easier language to express certain thoughts they had. But whenever they made Yiddish jokes and laughed, even when they explained them to Marilyn, she just sat at the table looking incredibly lonely, often with tears in her eyes.

"It was like when I was a little girl," she sobbed to me later one evening. "The families would talk and laugh and have fun with each other but not with me. I didn't belong and I knew it. I know they don't mean anything, but it's like . . . almost like being an orphan again." Although Mr. Miller's parents were particularly kind in teaching Marilyn Yiddish phrases and doing their best to make her feel like their "daughter," she still seemed to be distant, not a real part of their family.

I wondered when Marilyn and Arthur had the opportunity or the time to be romantic. He was always up well before she was. He had his own bathroom, kept his clothes in a separate hall closet, and virtually lived in his study. He rarely ventured into her bedroom during the day. Mr. Miller would usually have lunch alone, walked the dog by himself, and seemed to have more fun talking business with May Reis, about future projects for Marilyn, than talking to Marilyn herself.

Nevertheless, after some dinners, Marilyn would cuddle up to Mr. Miller, which always brought a big, boyish grin to his usually stern face. It was like the beautiful cheerleader had just fallen for the class genius, an unlikely pair but still a beaming one. And on certain mornings when I went in to change Marilyn's sheets, she would greet me with the biggest grin. "Wow!" she once explained, eyes glazed with a dreamy happiness, as she stretched and arched her back sensuously. "Don't change these, please," she said, rubbing her head along the sheets as if they were silk. "I want to lie on these all day."

"Didn't you sleep?" I asked, naively.

"Who said nights were for sleep," she winked. I knew she had enjoyed herself.

Evidently one night did produce the desired result. When Marilyn went to Hollywood to make her first movie in over a year, *Some Like It Hot,* she found out she was pregnant again. I remember her calling me long distance, squealing like a little girl. She asked me to start thinking about names, that she wanted me to make certain baby clothes, and that she knew it would be a girl.

I told Marilyn that I had wanted a girl, too, and that I was going to try again. "Good luck to both of us," she said. I myself got so excited that my sister and I went to a dozen or more stores to find Marilyn a gift. What we selected was a tiny, pink, handmade wooden crib, with a pink-cheeked baby girl in a bonnet under the covers. I put it on her night stand next to the pictures of her mother and Abraham Lincoln. When she came back from Hollywood and saw it, she cried and cried, and kissed me so much that I was afraid Mr. Miller might get jealous. It meant everything to her. From that day on, she began calling me "Baby Lamb." I don't know why, but that became her nickname for me. "Lena's not sweet enough for you," was all she said.

I had never seen her spirits so high. Although she had originally been opposed to *Some Like It Hot* on the dumb blonde grounds, as well as her dislike of its being filmed in black and white ("I'm better in color"), she now was overjoyed. The pregnancy made all the difference. She sang "I Wanna Be Loved By You," her big number from the picture, she raved about Jack Lemmon, and didn't even complain about Billy Wilder, about whom I would later hear the most unkind comments. She had also called me several other times from California, when they were filming at a beach resort near San Diego, talking about how good the sea and warm weather would be for her and the baby. "Nothing's gonna go wrong this time, Lena. Pray for me." I did.

When Marilyn returned from the *Some Like It Hot* filming, her high spirits had vanished. Now she began to panic that the baby wouldn't be all right. She tried to avoid her normal routine of champagne and sleeping pills. "I don't want to hurt the baby." Yet without these, she was terribly nervous. Normally, she would have paced about her bedroom, staring at herself in the mirrors, but this, too, she felt would disturb her baby. Instead, she just lay in bed, all alone, holding the little baby-in-the-cradle I had given her. Sometimes, when I would walk in to try to cheer her up, she would be lying on her side, the cradle right next to her head. She delicately pushed it around on the pillow next to her. A slow puddle of tears was building up next to it.

"What's wrong?" I asked.

"I'm so worried, Baby Lamb. In a way, I'm happy, but that's a bad sign. If I'm happy, I know something'll go wrong. I'm so cold." I got her some blankets and tucked her in.

Something did go wrong. One morning, Marilyn began screaming with intense pain. "I'm going to lose her," she shrieked. By noon Marilyn was so hysterical that we all knew this was not a typical depression. May Reis called the doctor, then an ambulance, and May and Mr. Miller rushed with Marilyn to the Polyclinic Hospital on Manhattan's West Side, near the theater district. I could hardly work, so worried about what might happen. Later that evening, Mr. Miller returned with the bad news. He was always serious and very composed, but this one time I sensed that he was fighting hard to avoid breaking down. When he told me that Marilyn had lost their baby, I started crying. Very kindly, he put his arm around my shoulder. We shared the same grief.

For two days, Marilyn was not allowed to have any visitors, but on the third day Marilyn called me herself from the hospital. "I'm starving, Baby Lamb. How about some chicken soup? I can't wait to see you." I cooked up a large pot, and was taken over to the hospital by the chauffeur. Marilyn was whiter than her plain white room. She looked the weakest I had ever seen her. She needed more than soup. Yet she pulled me over to her bed and kissed me. We didn't say much to each other, but we did cry a lot. "I can never have kids again, never," she sobbed.

"You can," I said. "I'm sure there's a way."

"I can't. Oh, Lena, I can't."

"Try to eat. At least you'll feel better."

She did manage to try the soup, and after the first few reluctant mouthfuls, she gulped down nearly the entire pot. "Gee, that's good," she said with a faint smile.

Two days later, when she was about to come home from the hospital, Marilyn called and asked me to go there again, this time with a beige coat and a low-cut beige silk dress that I was to pick up at Jax, a fancy store on Fifty-seventh Street where she bought many of her clothes. "I've got to look beautiful," she laughed.

"What for?"

"The reporters, who else?"

When I arrived at the hospital, Kenneth was also there working on her hair. Today's style was Marilyn's favorite—parted on the side, straight body, with a flip at the ends. She looked beautiful, in a tragic way, though. "You'd think I was going to a premiere," she said, then paused. "It's more like . . . like a funeral." Marilyn started crying again. I gave her her dark glasses to hide her reddened eyes, and we made our way down to the exit where the car was waiting. When we reached the door, a large group of reporters was there. They began to applaud. Instinctively, Marilyn waved and smiled at them. She was always a trouper, regardless of the circumstances. She didn't want to let her audience down. However, when we were in the limousine, she broke into tears again. "What were they cheering for? What's there to clap for? I lost my baby . . . that was my life."

"They were just being nice," I said. "Happy to see you well."

"I'm their freak," she moaned. "If only I had my baby and could tell the press to go to hell. I hate this. . . ." The car drove off, in a flash of cameras, toward East Fifty-seventh Street.

As soon as she reached her bedroom, she flung off her clothes and hopped into bed. She was wearing a pair of bloodstained underpants the hospital must have insisted on. "I have to wear these," she frowned. Mr. Miller stood by, very sober and concerned for a few minutes, and then returned to his study. He was to come out far more often in those posthospital days to check that Marilyn was all right. As Marilyn lay down, my heart nearly stopped. The little pink cradle was still on her night stand. In all the confusion, I had forgotten to hide it away. She noticed it immediately. At first she grabbed it and stared at it with a terrible longing. Then she hurled it across the room, breaking it and starting to cry bitterly. "Take it away. Take it. It's over. It's over. I can't." I gathered up the little pink cradle. The baby's head had broken off and lay on the floor. As I ran out, Marilyn called to me, "Baby Lamb, please, I'm sorry. I'm so sorry. I ain't got nothing anymore. I wanted . . . her . . . so bad. I'm sorry." I put the pieces of the toy in my room, and returned to her side, urging her to relax. "That was my last chance," she wept. "My last chance."

Despite the tender concern Mr. Miller showed to Marilyn in the month or so while she recuperated from her pregnancy, I got the feeling that the marriage was never again going to be the same. One clue came when Marilyn glanced around her room after her return. "It's so empty. No flowers. No get-well cards. Doesn't anybody care about me?" She said she knew that she didn't really have any friends of her own, "But what about Arthur?" She complained that Mr. Miller didn't have friends either. "What kind of life is this without friends? Without people? I never had any before, when I was little. But I thought I'd have some by now," she snapped bitterly.

Later, I suggested to Marilyn that she take a trip to Europe. That would have gotten her mind off all her problems about both babies and acting. Of course, I suggested a tour of Italy, starting with Lake Como in the Alps. "That's so romantic, you'll have another baby there in no time," I told her.

"Not with him," she laughed. "He won't go anywhere." I told her all about Venice, Florence, Rome, everywhere, and she got very excited. "Its like *Three Coins in the Fountain*," she said. "I saw that. You have to come, too," she insisted.

Regrettably, all this was just talk. "He won't go," she pouted, after she had pleaded with him several times for the trip. "He won't go anywhere. 'Got to write. Got to write,' " she mimicked him. "He's just a damn Communist. They won't let him go. That's why!" Marilyn was referring to Mr. Miller's problem in getting his passport to go to England for *The Prince and the Showgirl*. Because he had been involved in some supposedly left-wing political activities when he was younger, the government was suspicious of him.

I'm sure that now he was no more of a Communist than Marilyn, but calling him that was just a way for Marilyn to let off steam. "He's a big Communist. I can't go nowhere. Nowhere!" she fumed. But she never called Mr. Miller a Communist to his face. She was still very meek and humble in his presence. His calm dignity kept her in check; she was too embarrassed to have a fit in front of him.

At least for a while. Gradually, she became openly hostile. For example, one time, soon after Marilyn's hospital stay, several of the buttons fell off of one of Mr. Miller's favorite sport shirts. When he asked me if I could sew them back on for him, I told him I'd be glad to. However, Marilyn soon came into my room and saw me sewing on the buttons. "Why?" she asked, eyes bulging with a strange rage.

"Mr. Miller asked me to," I answered.

"We'll see about that." Marilyn yanked the shirt out of my hand. "Which buttons?" I showed her the ones. I couldn't figure out what was happening. Then she tore the buttons off and ran down the hall, nude, on into Mr. Miller's study. All I could hear was her screaming, "Lena works for me. Not you. For me. Leave her alone." When she returned, she was smiling ear to ear. "He won't do that to you again," Marilyn said, almost in triumph.

"Oh, but I didn't mind," I said.

"I do!" I didn't ask her why, but my expression must have been a big question mark; she felt she had to answer. "He won't do anything for me. He won't take me anyplace. He won't let me have any fun. So I won't do anything for him!" I was not used to seeing Marilyn being this stubborn, but it was clear that where Mr. Miller was concerned, she was highly agitated. I didn't dare try to argue with her.

Then came the bitter accusations of what Mr. Miller had done to Marilyn's career. "You let me be a dumb blonde in *Bus Stop*. You let Olivier make fun of me. You let them make *Some Like It Hot* in black and white." Even though Mr. Miller actually had had little to do with any of Marilyn's films, she needed a scapegoat to blame for what she considered her failures. Mr. Miller was the one. Furthermore, what had kept Mr. Miller so locked up in his study was that he was writing a screenplay for Marilyn based on his short story, *The Misfits*. He had originally written the story about some cowboys when he was in Nevada getting the divorce from his first wife. Although Marilyn hadn't studied her part (still incomplete), she was beginning to mistrust Mr. Miller here, too. "I bet he makes me another dumb blonde, just like the rest. Just wait."

Marilyn was getting a terrible chip on her shoulder against her husband. Once she even said, "He has his own kids. What does he care whether I have any?" Since I had seen the deep hurt in Mr. Miller's face when Marilyn had lost her baby, I tried to explain that I believed Mr. Miller did care about her. "Shit!" she snapped. "All he cares about is himself, his own writing. That's all. Who cares about me? Who?"

"I do."

"Oh, Baby Lamb, I know," Marilyn said, tears streaking her angry face. "You do. But who else?"

When I first began working for Marilyn, she had been attending a special English class. She had told me she wanted to learn to pronounce words right, to spell, to speak in correct sentences. Part of this was for her acting, but at least as much was to make Mr. Miller respect her more. "I may be blonde, but I'm sick of being dumb. I want him to be proud of me," she used to emphasize. Now, however, she stopped going to class. Her vocabulary became more and more obscene. Instead of her occasional "shit," she frequently cursed like a truck driver, even at the dinner table. Once she had an argument with Mr. Miller about *Some Like It Hot*, before it was released. She kept complaining about it. He tried to praise her for being funny. "Fuck you!" she shouted. "I don't want to be funny. Everyone's gonna laugh at me. And not because of my acting. I look like a fat pig. Those goddamn cocksuckers made me look like a funny fat pig. A freak. Funny! Shit!" Mr. Miller sat back quietly during the outburst; he seemed to realize there was nothing he could do. Meanwhile, Marilyn stabbed her fork into the spaghetti and ran into her bedroom, crying.

Mr. Miller's weekend retreat in Roxbury, Connecticut, didn't seem to provide a quiet getaway that would bring the couple together either. Frequently, they would drive out on Friday night and return on Sunday. Eventually, Marilyn would start going a day later, then often not at all. "I hate that place," she would say. "There's nothing to do." She didn't really do anything much on Fifty-seventh Street either, but at least she got phone calls there. She loved to talk on the phone. The times I visited the house in Connecticut the phone hardly rang at all.

At the farm, a plain house, the routine was very much the same as in New York. Mr. Miller would work—alone—on his writing, walk the dog, tend to his garden. Marilyn would stay in the bedroom, drink champagne, or sleep. The only times I saw her display any energy in Connecticut were the occasions when she invited my sons and husband out to spend Saturdays with her. There seemed to be no cooking at all at the farm, since either Hattie or I would have prepared enough food for the whole weekend. "Arthur makes eggs," Marilyn said. When my family arrived, Marilyn would run out to greet us, dressed for a change. She always wore some kind of casual cotton slacks and a blouse tied in a knot at her stomach. She was so happy, with her bright "Hi's" and kisses, that I thought we'd never get inside.

We'd usually enjoy a lunch of salami and cheese sandwiches on the porch. Marilyn washed hers down with champagne; we had Cokes. Mr. Miller never joined us at all. "Where's Mr. Miller?" I once asked.

"Where else?" Marilyn laughed, as she mimicked him intensely hunched over his books and papers. The few times we'd see him, he would smile a quick hello and return to his work. He never seemed to have time to chat.

Marilyn talked almost totally about us—Joe's job and my two boys. Their favorite activity was when Marilyn would put them on her pony. She walked the little horse around and around the big yard, as the boys took turns playing mounted cowboy. Marilyn was so good with both my boys, but it seemed as if she never would let go of my younger boy, Johnny, who was about six at the time. Johnny had very blonde hair, almost platinum, and Marilyn used to kiss him at least every five minutes. Sometimes my husband Joe would drive Marilyn, me, and the boys around the Connecticut hills to look at the country scenery and the leaves. During these trips, Marilyn would always hold Johnny in her lap. "I wish you could be mine," she told Johnny, as she nuzzled close to him.

"Me, too," Johnny said, "but I've already got a mommy!" Marilyn hugged him even closer, and smiled bravely, but I could see that the tears were beginning to flow. Later she told me that whenever she looked at Johnny, especially with that beautiful blonde hair, she thought about her own baby, the one that was taken from her. She hated when we had to go home, and always cried as we drove away.

Marilyn called both my sons her "little dolls" and was forever thanking me for "sharing them" with her. "It's as close to a mother as I'll ever be now," she wept. I begged her not to give up, and she didn't. However, after one more operation to try to improve her ability to have kids, the doctors apparently told her it was hopeless. This bad news saw her relationship with Mr. Miller grow even worse. If he couldn't be the father of her children, she didn't seem to be willing to accept him just as a husband. "I wanted a family," she said. "I hoped Arthur was going to give me a family. What else has he given me? Now I'll never have anything!" she despaired.

Marilyn's daily admiration of the picture of Joe DiMaggio in her closet seemed to increase. "Why, why did I ever let that get away?" she wondered aloud. "Stupid!" Otherwise, up until that point I had never known her to be anything but the most faithful wife. "Fooling around" never crossed her mind. What she wanted was the solid home life she thought a solid man like Mr. Miller was going to give her. She did love Mr. Miller, at least at first, but her pregnancy failures seemed to be the ruin of their relationship. They needed a child to hold them together.

Now I noticed that Marilyn had begun to think a little about new men and even to flirt with them. For example, one of the Puerto Rican handymen in the building always struck me as underfed. He was handsome, very dark, with nice features, but so skinny. One time he was working in the hall when a big bag of groceries arrived, and I never saw a man look so hungry. When I told Marilyn about this, she insisted,

"Let's feed him!" Then she asked, "Is he cute?" When I said yes, she said, "Let him eat with me." I made him a big bowl of pasta and a steak and served him in Marilyn's bedroom. She wore her white robe, very loosely draped about her, and clearly enjoyed the man's dazzled look. He couldn't make up his mind whether to eat his steak or stare at Marilyn. He left happy, though, and we prepared a tray for him as long as he was with the building.

Sometimes Marilyn would take me with her to Bloomingdale's to look at clothes, mostly sportswear. There, Marilyn seemed to get a big kick when people, especially men, noticed her. Even though she'd be wearing a scarf, dark glasses, and sometimes a black wig, somehow Marilyn came through. She loved to wink and even flirt with her admirers in the store, asking them if this blouse or that one made her look "too fat." All the men could say was, "You're beautiful," even if she had the blouse on upside down. It was funny. She would do this until the crowd started growing and made her want to dash off. "I don't want to answer any questions," she'd tell me as we'd run for a back stairway to get to the waiting limousine. Other times, she'd stare at movie posters, almost like a star-struck fan herself. "Wow! He's handsome," she would exclaim as she admired the pictures of actors, especially young, new faces I had never seen before.

Marilyn even liked to flirt with my husband. She knew that I was too close a friend to get jealous, and she also knew Joe thoroughly enjoyed being in her company. He always teased her about the "serious actress" business. "Be sexy," he said. "You're the sexiest woman in the world. What do you want to play? An old lady? Hey, what's wrong with you?"

He made Marilyn laugh. "It's Arthur," she'd half-apologize. "You know, he's a big writer and all. Very serious. I can't go out and act like a . . . you know . . . a dumb blonde. That'd make him look silly."

Joe just laughed. "Be yourself. He loves you for yourself," he'd say.

The thing about Joe that intrigued Marilyn the most was his tattoos, which he had gotten during the war. He had them on his arms, on his chest, on his back, all over. Marilyn was forever rolling up his sleeves and examining each tattoo, closely. Some of them were very elaborate, and she found them fascinating. One evening, Joe and Marilyn were sitting in the kitchen while I was making lasagna. She couldn't control her curiosity. "Joe . . . could you . . . could you show me all your tattoos?"

"All?"

Marilyn got red and giggled. "Yeah, all of them. I really like them."

Joe thought for a second. Then a devilish grin lit up his face. "Is Mr. Miller here?" he asked. Marilyn said he was away. "O.K., then. You really want to see?"

"Yes, yes," Marilyn said, like a little girl.

"O.K. You make me a deal. And I make you a deal."

"Sure," Marilyn said. "What do you want me to do?"

"Well, all the guys at my job don't believe that my wife works for you, and I said I'd prove it. How? With an autographed pair of your panties! But they don't want you to just take them out of the closet and sign them. They want you to take them off, the ones you're wearing now, and sign *them*. You know about how guys are. . . ."

"Lena, is that all right with you?" Marilyn asked.

"Oh, sure," I said, "we're all one big family." I

had told Joe Marilyn didn't wear panties, but he didn't believe me.

"O.K., Joe," Marilyn smiled wickedly, "but first you take off your shirt."

"You promise you're not teasing me?" Joe said.

"Promise."

Joe took off his shirt, to reveal an eye-popping array of tattoos. Marilyn couldn't take her eyes away, tracing all the ships and stuff with her fingers, all over his chest and back. I think Joe was getting a little excited waiting for his end of the bargain. "Your turn," he said.

"Oh," Marilyn whispered, "I forgot to tell you, I don't have any panties."

"There you go. I knew it. I knew I'd get taken for a ride!" Joe laughed.

"No, really," Marilyn said. "I never lie. Look!" Marilyn lifted up her white dress and showed Joe that she wasn't wearing anything at all. He nearly fainted. Marilyn and I burst out laughing. She opened a little bottle of Piper for Joe. "Here, you need it." They toasted each other.

Then Marilyn ran back to her bedroom. When she returned, she tapped a still stunned Joe on the shoulder. He turned around, and immediately she flashed up her skirt again, to reveal a pair of bright red panties. "Like these?"

"Jesus!" he said, gulping down the rest of his champagne. Since I had never seen Marilyn wear panties before, I hadn't realized she could have so much fun with underwear. Soon she balanced herself on one leg, then another, and took the panties off. With a pen I handed her, she autographed them, "To Joe, with much love, Marilyn."

"I won't ask if you have any other tattoos," Marilyn smiled, shooting a mischievous glance at Joe's slacks. He was too dazed even to notice. He took the panties to work the next day. "That made me the king out there. The King." He never stopped boasting about the story.

"I wish Arthur felt like that," Marilyn said later. "I bet you and Joe have a good time. He's a great man." I just laughed.

In any event, after more than a year with Marilyn, I found her dissatisfied with almost every part of her life. She wasn't seeming to master becoming a "serious dramatic actress." She couldn't have children. She and Mr. Miller weren't getting along. She wasn't taking advantage of New York. Marilyn was never more unhappy; her favorite companions were champagne and sleeping pills. Her psychiatrists didn't seem to have the right answer for her. Except for the Strasbergs, she had not made any new friends who could help her. Yet with the release of *Some Like It Hot,* she was to become a bigger star than ever before, though that success meant little to her. Every day Marilyn was either angry, hysterical, or both. I was very worried about her.

6

Some Like It Hot was Marilyn's most successful movie. The audiences loved it. The critics loved it. All the people she knew, including Mr. Miller, loved it. Marilyn hated it. And the thing she hated most was the film's very success, for now people were saying that no one had ever played a "dumb blonde" more perfectly. "That's it!" she screamed for months after the film's release. "I'm stuck. I'm a dumb blonde forever now. I've ruined everything for myself!"

Marilyn was against the project almost from the beginning. It was now 1958, and she hadn't made a movie since *The Prince and the Showgirl*, in the summer of 1956. However, she wasn't in any rush. Scripts would pour into the house for her consideration, but the only ones who seemed to consider them were May Reis and Mr. Miller. They would go over the screenplays very carefully and then give Marilyn the few that they thought she would like. They were always wrong. Marilyn would usually read a couple of pages and then toss the script in a corner. "Another stupid girl. I can't stand it," she would complain. "Don't you know what I want?" Sometimes, if she saw a certain director's name connected with a script, she would refuse to read it at all. "He'd never give me a fair chance," she'd say. "If I have to wait for the role I want, I'll just wait. I don't care."

One day, however, Mr. Miller and May seemed to be very excited about, not a script, but a several-page outline of a proposed movie. Mr. Miller talked to Marilyn for a long time about the idea, and she agreed this would be her next movie. That night she told me about it. "I'm going to play the lead singer in an all-girl band. During Prohibition, you know, in the twenties with all the gangsters." She wasn't really sure what the story was. What impressed her most was that the film was going to be directed by Billy Wilder, who had brought her such success in *The Seven Year Itch*.

"He's the best director in Hollywood," she praised him. "He's the cleverest, too. Billy's funny and smart." She said that Billy Wilder appreciated her more than any other director did. "There's no question who's the star if I'm in his movie." This new project seemed like the perfect way for Marilyn to make her screen comeback. She believed that the director was the most important person in shaping a movie and making it work, and she had total confidence that she had one who understood her. Besides, she would get to sing. "Singing makes me a lot less nervous than acting," she said. And, above all, it was hinted that Frank Sinatra might be in the film. "Oh, Frankie," she beamed, "that would be so much fun, I wouldn't care *what* the movie was about."

Her enthusiasm disappeared the moment she read

the entire script, sometime later. Then she learned that the story was actually about two musicians who have witnessed a gangland murder. They flee Chicago and the mob by dressing up as women and joining Marilyn's all-girl band. "That's ridiculous!" Marilyn shrieked when she finally figured out what the plot was. "I've been dumb, but never *that* dumb. How *couldn't* I recognize that they were men? I won't do it. Never!" She hurled the script across the room.

Although Mr. Miller tried, very calmly, to convince Marilyn what a great opportunity the film was, she didn't want to listen. He evidently suggested that she could make a fortune from the project and that they could use the money. Despite the fact that neither of them had been working, the mere mention of money set Marilyn off. "All he cares about is money. Not me! Money!" she cried to me. "That's all that matters. Why doesn't he try to write something he hates? Then he'd see. I can't take another one of these parts. This is the dumbest ever." Marilyn began throwing blame on everyone—Mr. Miller, her lawyers, her agents, anyone connected with movies as a "business." Marilyn simply didn't want to think about money. "I trust these guys . . . I pay them . . . to take care of money, and look what they do. Trick me into this."

Marilyn was in a blind rage for days. All she did was eat. I never saw anyone eat so much. One day she had three eggs and toast, three hamburgers, three plates of home fries, two chocolate milk shakes, a big veal cutlet, two helpings of eggplant parmigiana, and four cups of chocolate pudding, all washed down with champagne and all in her bedroom—alone. She was still so hungry that she ran in and out of the kitchen, nude, while Hattie or I would be cooking, asking, "Isn't it ready yet?" and nibbling at whatever was lying on the counter.

I teased her about her endless desire for the chocolate pudding. "That's baby food," I said.

"Baby elephant," she laughed. "I'm going to get so fat they won't let me be in this awful picture."

No matter what Marilyn ate and how fat she was getting, no one stopped wanting her. Despite her reservations, she eventually signed the contract to make *Some Like It Hot*. Aside from the food, the thing that calmed her the most was the songs she found out she'd be singing in the movie. She loved to sing, and did it well. Between meals, she'd sit in the bed, strumming her new ukulele that she was to learn to play, practicing the lyrics. When she was unhappy, she'd stick with "I'm Through with Love." But most often she sang "I Wanna Be Loved by You."

Marilyn was most disappointed when she learned that Frank Sinatra would not be in the movie. Evidently, Billy Wilder had tried, but was unable to get him. Her two co-stars would instead be Jack Lemmon and Tony Curtis. While she didn't know either of them well, she kept talking about how handsome Tony Curtis was. That, at least, was something she had to look forward to. Still, she would have occasional spells of cold feet when she would cry and beg Mr. Miller not to "make her" go to Hollywood for the movie. He never lost his patience, always trying to explain to her that the movie depended on her and that only she could make it a hit.

I am not sure that she would have ever gone through with it, though, if she wasn't guaranteed to have Paula Strasberg by her side at all times as her dramatic coach. "Just 'cause I'm in another comedy won't prevent me from becoming a serious dramatic actress someday," Marilyn told me. It was an attempt to persuade herself the movie wouldn't hurt her future as an artist. That it stood to make her rich financially couldn't have mattered less. Once I said to her, to try to cheer her up, that she should start planning all the nice things she would buy with the money she made from the movie. "Lena," she said, "I don't want anything. Not things. I've got things. I just want to have a real career. I want to act. I want friends. I want to be happy. I want some respect. I don't want to be laughed at. Doesn't anyone understand?"

I am not sure how much Mr. Miller and Marilyn had saved from their earlier works, but it never occured to her that money was necessary just to keep her household going. The staff, the beauty people, the clothes, the champagne, the doctors, the rent, altogether must have cost a great deal. Yet Marilyn assumed that plenty of money was there. If she was so famous, how could she be poor, she thought. "I worried about money for too long," she said. "I'm sick of it. I am never going to worry about it again." Whenever Mr. Miller or May Reis tried to discuss finances with her, she would put her hands over her ears and turn away.

Marilyn's misgivings about *Some Like It Hot* seemed to make everyone concerned with the project very nervous. One day, Marilyn had Kenneth and her makeup girls around to fix her up early in the morning. That day, Marilyn said, Billy Wilder, Jack Lemmon, and Tony Curtis were coming up together to the apartment to talk about the film. She wanted to look good, especially for Tony Curtis. "He's married to Janet Leigh. She's beautiful," Marilyn said admiringly. She wanted to make a good impression. Also, she mentioned that Billy Wilder was the most critical man in Hollywood when it came to women's beauty. "When he looks at you, you know he's noticing everything that's wrong."

I must have ironed ten blouses that day. Every one

was wrong. Once I thought she had finally selected one, but she couldn't make up her mind how many buttons to leave undone. The problem, as she put it, was "either my breasts fall out or I look too prissy." She selected another blouse, a tight white silk one, which went nicely with her checked slacks. "Are they tight enough?" she asked constantly, not worrying that they might be *too* tight. I assured her the men would love her.

When Marilyn's guests arrived in midafternoon, she was still dressing and undressing. She asked me to go out and help them get drinks. For three men who were putting together what would become one of the funniest movies ever made, I had never seen anyone looking less in the mood for laughs. The three were almost identically dressed, in dark business suits and ties. They looked serious, and nervous. The one Marilyn said was Billy Wilder certainly didn't look like the man with the sharpest eyes for women in Hollywood. He was bald, paunchy, and wore glasses. (I guess I had expected a dashing Cecil B. De Mille, with boots, breeches, and dark glasses.) The three men looked more like undertakers than comedians. While they waited for Marilyn, they fidgeted in their seats and kept whispering to each other things like, "Make sure she knows she's the star," "Push the singing," and "Be positive."

When Marilyn at last burst into the room with a smiling "Hi," the very straight faces quickly lit up, too. There was a lot of hugging and kissing, which, Marilyn told me later, was standard Hollywood behavior, even if the people hardly knew each other. Then they talked about the movie for over an hour. Whenever Marilyn expressed her doubts, especially that no one could believe that the men's female disguises would work, the three men would take turns assuring her that the public would believe them, as long as Marilyn did. "But I don't," Marilyn said. "How can I?" Then they told her that she was a great actress and only she could convince the audience. The whole movie depended on her, they kept repeating. The discussion ended with lots of laughter and lots of kissing.

Yet, no sooner than she had said the warmest good-bye, Marilyn rushed back to her room, ripped her clothes off, and started crying. "Champagne, Lena, quick," she called out.

"What's wrong?" I asked. "Didn't you have fun with them?"

"Fun? Shit! Business, nothing but business. They have to have me. Sure. 'Cause I'm the only one who could be dumb enough to believe those guys were girls. Why do I have to act dumb? Can't I do something else? Anything?"

I had never seen Marilyn more miserable. Her depression over *Some Like It Hot* might have never ended had she not found out that she was pregnant (with the baby she would lose at the end of the filming). This changed her spirits altogether. Suddenly, she became happy and optimistic. She never sang "I'm Through with Love" anymore. She even stopped dreaming about Joe DiMaggio. And as for *Some Like It Hot,* she agreed to go through with it. "I don't like it," she said, "but it's not worth hurting the baby getting all upset about it. It's just another movie, another job," she shrugged. "This is what matters," Marilyn said proudly, patting her stomach.

Unfortunately, once Marilyn and Mr. Miller arrived in Hollywood for the filming in late summer, 1958, the aggravation began again. They stayed at the Beverly Hills Hotel, Marilyn's favorite. However, outside the hotel and on the set, Marilyn was afraid that the whole film crew was conspiring to humiliate her. Marilyn called me every couple of nights to tell me about how frightening everything seemed to her. She felt all alone, except for Paula Strasberg. "You and Paula, you're the only ones who care, Baby Lamb. I can't talk to these people out here. To them, I'm a fool. They're out to use me. If Paula wasn't here to stand up for me, I'd quit and come home," she whispered on the phone in the saddest voice.

The first big crisis occurred when Marilyn found out that the film was being made in black and white. She felt that she looked much better in color and thought that a guarantee that each of her films be shot in color had been in her contract. It wasn't. Although she told me that Billy Wilder's excuse was that the men in drag would look totally ridiculous if they were in color, especially in their makeup, Marilyn felt betrayed. "They're ridiculous anyway," she fumed. "Now *I'm* going to look ridiculous! They said it was supposed to be my movie, but it's *his*."

"His" referred to Billy Wilder. Gradually, the man she admired as the smartest in Hollywood became, in her mind, her worst enemy. She started calling him "little Hitler." She admitted that Mr. Miller had scolded her for this. Wilder may have been German, but he wasn't little and he was Jewish. It was wrong to call him Hitler, but Marilyn was so frustrated, she wasn't thinking. "I don't care what he is, he's a 'little Hitler' to me. He's not a director, he's a dictator. He doesn't care about anyone's feelings. All he cares about is his damn movie."

Because of her great concern for the baby, Marilyn wanted to be sure she got enough sleep. And because she had trouble falling asleep, to get enough meant she sometimes had to sleep until noon. Perhaps Billy Wilder and the others didn't realize at the time that

Marilyn was pregnant. But pregnant or not, Marilyn received little sympathy from Wilder. He was a professional, who believed in being on time, not to mention the pressures upon him to make the movie within its budget. Marilyn knew that her lateness may have been inconveniencing the entire cast and delaying production, but for her, the baby came first, no matter what. The baby was the one thing she had been desperate to have for so long. Her dream now seemed possible. She wasn't going to take any risks at all.

Another problem she told me about was Wilder's impatience that she took so long to do a scene right. "Right for him means exactly by the script. *His* script. I might think of a better way, but unless it's *his* way, he makes me do it over and over." One time she said she had to repeat a scene over fifty times. Sometimes, she herself would insist on doing a scene over, to get it as close to perfect as possible. "I don't like my job here, but I wanted to do it as well as I can. Everybody's gonna see me, so I've *got* to be good," she told me sincerely. But Wilder's ideas of perfection were often not the same as Marilyn's, and he seemed, to her, to get annoyed whenever she tried to assert her judgment.

The only scene she enjoyed repeating was the one on a yacht, where she seduced Tony Curtis, who in the movie has fallen in love with Marilyn's character, Sugar Kane. Shedding his girl disguise, he pretends he's a millionaire and sneaks aboard the yacht of a real millionaire. The real millionaire is away, chasing Jack Lemmon—that is, the girl Jack Lemmon is posing as. To win Sugar's sympathy, Tony Curtis tells her that he has problems with women and that he can't get excited by them. Sugar falls for the story and does all she can to "cure him." "She was so-o-o dumb," Marilyn giggled over the phone, describing the scene. She told

me she had to kiss Tony Curtis, many, many times and
that "it was fun." Aside from her singing, it was the
only good thing she had to say about the movie.

Marilyn assumed that Tony Curtis had fun, too.
She later heard that when someone asked him how he
liked kissing Marilyn, he said it was like kissing Hitler.
She was crushed. Now *she* was being compared to
Hitler, and by an actor she thought much of. Tony
Curtis seemed to have been drained by Marilyn's
lateness and countless extra "takes." He lost his
temper. But now instead of praising him, Marilyn
criticized him for being so cynical and made fun of
what she called his "Brooklyn accent." She tried to
mock him by lowering her voice and speaking in a
gruff, New York cabdriver way. Although she lost her
affection for Tony Curtis, she came to like Jack Lemmon more and more. "He's one of the nicest guys I've
ever met," she said. "He understands how scared I
am in front of the cameras. He's scared, too, and he's
not ashamed of it. He tells me. That helps a lot."

Although her first instinct was to like everyone,
Marilyn was incredibly quick to sense if someone
didn't like her. The minute she got this negative feeling, she would drop the person immediately, no matter
how friendly he or she may have been in the past.
"You can only give so much of yourself," Marilyn
wept to me after hearing the Tony Curtis story. "I try
to give to everyone, but a person only has so much
affection. I'm not going to waste mine on anyone
who's against me. From now on, I'm saving my
friendship for people who care. This movie's a nightmare, Lena."

Marilyn's nightmare got even worse. As soon as
she finished the film, which was over a month behind
schedule, she came home to rest. But soon she lost her

baby, despite every effort in the world to have it. Of course, she blamed everything on *Some Like It Hot,* on Billy Wilder, and on Mr. Miller for letting her go through with it. She was terribly upset and understandably so.

As if her luck wasn't bad enough, the movie continued to curse her. Shortly after her miscarriage, while she was trying to recuperate, an interview with Billy Wilder appeared in a New York newspaper. In it, Wilder made a lot of jokes about Marilyn's being late and not knowing her lines. He said she had made him sick and implied that he would never work with her again. When Marilyn heard about the interview, she insisted that May Reis get the paper and read it to her. May read it aloud several times. Then Marilyn read it herself. She couldn't believe that Billy Wilder would make fun of her in public, not after what she had just gone through. "*I* made *him* sick!" she shouted, ripping the newspaper apart. "*I* made *him* sick!"

Despite her doctor's orders to rest, she leaped out of bed and ran into Mr. Miller's study. "It's your fault!" I could hear her scream at him, all through the apartment. "You *do* something about it. . . . What do you mean, 'What can you do?' . . . You *have* to do something! *Say* something! Now everybody in the world'll take me for a fool. You've got to say something. People'll listen to *you. You've* got respect. . . . Forget it?" she shrieked. "Forget it! I'll never forget it. I'll never forget my baby. . . . *Say* something! . . . If you love me, you'll do it."

After a while, Mr. Miller put his arm around Marilyn and helped her back to her room. He was very disturbed about her. He couldn't stand noise and fighting, and I could tell that he really did hope she would go to sleep and forget the whole thing. Several times that day, she got hysterical, running in and out of his study screaming, and pulling her hair out. She was insisting that Mr. Miller speak out on her behalf. That night I prepared an Italian dinner for the couple, but neither one came to the table or ate anything at all. Marilyn just lay in her bed, sobbing and drinking champagne.

Eventually, Mr. Miller did speak out. He sent Billy Wilder a number of telegrams protesting the director's comments and praising Marilyn's work. Yet the telegrams Billy Wilder sent back made Marilyn still more upset. Wilder was making a joke out of the whole thing. He closed one telegram with the last and most famous line from *Some Like It Hot*, "Nobody's perfect." This was what the eccentric millionaire had said to Jack Lemmon when Lemmon pulled off his wig and revealed that he was a man. Neither Marilyn nor Mr. Miller saw any humor in this, but they realized that nothing more could be said. Marilyn's once favorite director now was the symbol of all she hated in Hollywood. She vowed she'd never work with him or talk to him again.

In the winter of 1959, Marilyn gradually forgot her bitter experience with *Some Like It Hot*. She considered other projects, she rested and she ate. And ate. She got up to nearly 140 pounds. Her normal weight was 115. In some ways, she resembled a powerful football player more than a movie star. I was delighted to cook, if that made Marilyn happy, or at least helped her forget the past. Fat or skinny, she still was beautiful. After several months and many pounds, I was relieved that we had heard the last of *Some Like It Hot*. However, in March, many people began calling Marilyn about attending the film's world premiere, which was to be held on Broadway. The people behind the film were especially anxious that she go. The publicity of her appearance, they told her, would be very valuable for the film's financial success.

I immediately assumed that she would refuse. She did at first. But not for the reasons I expected. Marilyn was refusing to go, not for her bad memories of the filming, not for her dislike of Billy Wilder, not to demonstrate her disgust with playing dumb blondes. She didn't want to go because she felt she was too fat. "I look terrible, and it's too late to lose weight," she said frantically. "I can't go out in public looking like this. Not to a premiere."

The phone calls didn't stop. "They tell me I'm more voluptuous than ever," Marilyn said in an annoyed tone that underscored the word "voluptuous." "They'll say anything to get me to go. What do you think?"

"I think they're right," I said. "You can look sexier now than ever. The more the better."

"You really think so? You think I can go out?"

"Sure. Why not?"

Mr. Miller and May Reis encouraged Marilyn, too, by assuring her she looked good. I think that she was looking for encouragement, and she really wanted to go very much. "At least I can dress up and get out of this damned apartment," Marilyn said. The kind words worked. Marilyn agreed to go.

The unseasonably warm day of the premiere at the end of March was one of the most hectic of my entire time with Marilyn. It was hectic for everyone, beginning with Kenneth. He must have tried every hairstyle he knew on Marilyn, but none would satisfy her. They all made her look "too fat," she moaned. By midafternoon, she finally settled upon a curly style that made her then platinum-colored hair look particularly radiant. Kenneth, May, Hattie, Mr. Miller, and I were all consulted, and we all approved loudly. When I gave her my compliment, Marilyn gave me a disgusted glare. "You're just being nice, Lena. I look like a fat whore, I know it, but it's too late to change now."

Several makeup people spent hours on their work, while Marilyn drank bottle after bottle of champagne. She refused to eat all day. "So my stomach'll be flat," she said, fighting a losing battle. She was worried about drinking so much. "What if I have to get up during the picture and go to the bathroom? I don't want the photographers to see me standing up any more than possible," she fretted. "Oh, the hell with it. If I don't drink, I'll be too nervous to go."

Marilyn had told me many times how frightened the whole film business made her. She felt terrible jitters in front of the live cameras, even worse in front of crowds. The only time she felt relaxed and sure of herself was before a still camera. "I love photographs," she said. "No lines. No acting. Just one guy and me. That's enough. That's good."

At around six o'clock Marilyn had finally selected a low-cut, strapless gown to wear, after agonizing over several. Even though I had let it out as far as it would go, it looked as if it would burst at the seams. Marilyn knew it, as she spun around time and again before the mirror, trying to convince herself the dress fit right. "How did I let myself get this way?" Marilyn cried aloud. "How? Look at my arms. Ugh! I wish it was winter. I wish I could wear sleeves."

May Reis, who was nervously watching at the door, worried that Marilyn might be late. Usually, she kept her remarks completely to herself, but for some reason she blurted out, "Nobody asked you to eat so much. You knew the premiere would be in the spring."

Marilyn could make all the negative comments she wanted to about herself. That didn't bother her. But when someone else criticized her, she fell apart. No sooner had May spoken than a horrified look came over her face. May should have held her tongue. Poor Marilyn burst into tears and fell on the bed. "I'm not going. I look like a freak. I'm not going." May ran for Mr. Miller, who tried to quiet Marilyn down.

Nothing seemed to work. Even the normally un- ruffled Mr. Miller just stood there, puffing on his pipe, anxiously buttoning and unbuttoning his tuxedo jacket. He and May exchanged hopeless glances. Meanwhile, Marilyn kept crying, her elaborate makeup running all over her sheets. When the others left the room, I found a silver lamé gown with a plunging V-neckline and spaghetti straps and laid it beside her on the bed. "This one's for you," I said. "Now come on. Half of New York's waiting for you. And all my family's going to be there, too." She had gotten us all seats near her. "They've been looking forward to this. You won't let them down."

"Me?" She looked up, her face all puffy from crying. "They want me?"

"Of course. They can see the stupid movie any- time, but they can't see you. This is a big treat for them. They love you. Now wear this. You'll look great."

"Oh, Baby Lamb, you know I'd never let you down." Marilyn immediately got up and changed, calling her makeup girls back for some retouching. She felt a real duty to her fans. And since she had person- ally invited my husband, my sons, and our relatives, she felt a special responsibility to them. Marilyn was one person who always kept her promises, even if giving in to herself and staying home would have been a far easier thing to do. She was a real friend, and I was very proud of her.

Marilyn had a hard time squeezing into the new

dress I had selected, but once in, she looked sexier
than ever before. The extra weight didn't even matter;
in fact, it really made her more alluring as a sex
goddess. Marilyn may not have wanted to be thought
of that way. Still, she certainly looked the part now.
When she insisted on drinking one more split of champagne before she left, Mr. Miller kept pacing outside
her bedroom, saying, "Come on. Come on." His
usually steel nerves had for once gotten the better of
him.

Finally, we all got into the elevator. But when we
reached the lobby, Marilyn realized that she had forgotten the little cap she wore between her front teeth
to disguise a space there. A distressed Mr. Miller
gnashed his teeth, as Marilyn and I went back upstairs
to get it. Before coming down again, she sneaked one
last gulp of champagne and a long look in the mirror.
"I hope they like me," she said.

"They will," I promised her.

Mr. Miller and Marilyn went to the theater in their
limousine, while my family and I followed in a cab.
Marilyn had gotten us seats in the row behind her.
"Listen to what everyone says and tell me everything.
The truth, O.K.?" she had directed me. When we all
arrived, a huge crowd was cheering for Marilyn. She
may have been scared, but her big smile and friendly
waving concealed her fear very well. We were all
hurried to our seats. Marilyn, who had been drinking
all day, nearly fell over several times. "Walk straight.
Walk straight," Mr. Miller whispered as he held her up
by the arm. Every eye in the audience was on Marilyn,
though she tried to pretend she was merely another
moviegoer. She turned back to look at me, with a big
grin. "Well, here goes, Baby Lamb. Wish me luck."
She reached out to grasp my hand for assurance and
blew kisses to my little boys.

"Good luck, Marilyn," they said, blowing kisses back. That made her the happiest she had been all day.

Marilyn watched the movie closely and laughed at all the jokes, even those of Tony Curtis. That is, until she appeared. Immediately, she grimaced with a loud "Oh!" and covered her eyes with her hands, peeking out only when she knew she wasn't on camera. It was like watching a horror movie with a queasy stomach. Every bad memory was right there on the screen, just to torture her. Several times she turned around to me with a pained expression that said, "This is awful. I told you so." It so happened that in every scene Marilyn was in, the audience was going wild with laughter. She didn't smile once, and kept covering her face. It didn't occur to her that the people were laughing because she was a great comedienne. In her mind, they were laughing because she, Marilyn, not Sugar, was dumb. And fat.

During the yacht scene with Tony Curtis, Marilyn wouldn't look at all. The audience was going wild, both over Tony Curtis's phony "sex troubles" and Marilyn's see-through dress.

Marilyn couldn't stand it. Mr. Miller put his arm around her almost as if to keep her from running out of the theater. In fact, the only scenes with herself she would watch were those when she sang. With her first song, "Running Wild," she became a different woman altogether. She smiled with self-satisfaction at how well she performed. The fact that the audience didn't laugh at her then made her feel even better. When she finished "I'm Through with Love," she turned around and gave my family a cute wink. Then the laughs began again and up went Marilyn's hands.

At the end of the movie, the audience stood and cheered wildly. It was a great success. Yet Marilyn didn't care. She rushed out of the theater, Mr. Miller struggling to keep up with her. There wasn't a word for reporters as she slammed the door to her limousine and was driven away. When the reporters started asking me about my boss, I gave them a "no comment" answer. Marilyn had warned me many times never to say anything to reporters. "They'll just change it around and make fun of all of us," she had cautioned me.

When I arrived back at the apartment, Marilyn was throwing a fit. "Disgusting! Disgusting! Disgusting!" she kept repeating. She had taken off her dress, leaving it on the floor, and had messed up her hair with her fingers. She was running in and out of the kitchen with a champagne bottle in her hand, yelling, "Disgusting!"

Mr. Miller tried to tell her that she was great and that she should try to be happy with her success.

"Shut up," she barked at him, driving him back behind the closed door of the study. "Lena," she ran to me the moment I came in, "did you see how fat I was? Like a pig. Oh, God! Wasn't that movie terrible?"

"No. It was fantastic. So were you." I had to tell the truth.

"You, too?" She took my praise like a stab in the back. "You!" She ran into her room and locked the door. I knocked several times to no answer. After having no luck in getting her to talk, I went home. It had been a long day.

The next morning when I arrived, Marilyn was still locked in. When I asked from outside if she was all right, she answered, "I can't talk. I can't stand it. Yesterday was a disaster for me." Soon, however, the phone calls started coming with news of the great reviews for the movie and the acclaim for Marilyn's performance. Later, she let May Reis in to show her what the critics had said. That made her feel a little better, but she was still disturbed about her appearance. "No more food!" she exclaimed. "I'm never going to eat again." That very day she went on a strict diet of fruits, vegetables, and, only on occasion, an egg. She could have incredible discipline when she wanted to.

Later, Marilyn called me to talk. "What did they say? What did you hear the people at the movie say, Lena?" Marilyn asked. Despite the critics' praise, she was even more concerned with what the average people in the audience thought. While the comment I overheard most was, "This is the perfect role for her," I didn't dare tell Marilyn this. Not now. I told her only that they loved the movie and they loved her.

"All these people are calling me and telling me how beautiful I looked," Marilyn said. "But they all work for me in some way. When I pay somebody a lot of money, they're not going to tell me I'm fat and ugly."

"Gee, you're pretty smart today," I teased her. We started laughing together.

Although the movie would make her a fortune and make her even more famous all over the world, Marilyn never again mentioned the words *Some Like It Hot*.

7

After the agonies of *Some Like It Hot,* I thought for a time that Marilyn would never make a movie again. She seemed to hate Hollywood more than ever and frequently spoke about doing a Broadway play with the Strasbergs. Yet her mind seemed to change a few months later when she received an acting award from the Italian movie industry for her performance in *The Prince and the Showgirl.* Nothing could have made Marilyn happier or boosted her self-confidence more than to be recognized as an actress. "Only the Italians appreciate me," she joked. "You, Frankie, Joe, and now this. What's wrong with Hollywood?"

I went with Marilyn to the Italian consulate on Park Avenue to receive her award. She wanted me to be her interpreter, in case she needed one. She wore a black cocktail dress, with a matching black jacket and black patent-leather, high-heel shoes. Still on her fruit and vegetable diet, she was now down into the upper 120s.

She looked very good and quite sedate in her black outfit. It was a far cry from her typical low necklines and skintight fits. "The Italian men are going to be disappointed," I laughed.

"Oh, Lena, it's a big award. It's like an Oscar. I don't want to be disrespectful." I could see how proud she was of the honor.

There was a champagne reception for Marilyn at the consulate, with about fifty dignitaries in attendance. One of the people there was the great actress Anna Magnani, who was one of the biggest stars in Italy. I had always admired her. As the crowd pressed around Marilyn, Anna Magnani stood by herself in a corner, sipping champagne and getting madder and madder by the minute. Obviously, she wasn't used to not being the center of attention and her feelings were hurt. Soon she reached her breaking point. She started to storm out, but had to fight through the mob admiring Marilyn in order to find an exit.

Anna Magnani completely lost her temper. She began cursing Marilyn in Italian and making fun of her countrymen as fools for paying so much attention to a woman who couldn't even act. *"Putane!"* she shouted as she left. *"Putane!"* This means whore in Italian, and I was glad that Marilyn didn't understand the language. Her outburst didn't faze Marilyn at all. She was getting too much pleasure from her own recognition. "What was wrong with her?" Marilyn asked me on the way home.

"She was just jealous. She was used to always being the star," I said.

"Oh, I know. These women movie stars never get along with me. They hate me on sight, so I've given up trying to make them like me."

One woman movie star, however, was responsible for changing Marilyn's views about money and, in effect, driving Marilyn back to Hollywood. This was Elizabeth Taylor. Marilyn always felt inferior to her, standing in awe of Taylor's English background, her voice, her more refined manner. Nonetheless, Marilyn felt competitive with Elizabeth Taylor as a star. When she heard Taylor was getting a million dollars to make *Cleopatra*, she was outraged.

What bothered her most was that Taylor's huge fee was coming from Marilyn's studio, Twentieth Century-Fox. "What do I get?" Marilyn asked May Reis. Marilyn received only a hundred thousand dollars a picture. It seemed like a fortune to me, but to Marilyn, it now seemed like nothing. She was insulted. Was she only one-tenth as valuable as Elizabeth Taylor?

After frantic calls to her lawyers and agents, Marilyn learned that she had a contract with Twentieth Century that obligated her to make four films for the company for that amount. Then she could be free to command a far higher salary, higher than Elizabeth Taylor's, her business agents assured her. Marilyn quickly decided that she wanted to make those movies and get them over with. "How can I be getting so little?" she puzzled over and over. Marilyn had plenty of money. And as long as she kept making movies she was sure to become a millionaire, regardless of how freely she spent. But now, for the first time, money took on an important symbolic value to Marilyn. She wanted to be the "biggest" star, and the biggest star, as she saw it, got the biggest salary.

Consequently, she rushed into a new project which Twentieth Century-Fox had suggested to her. "Let's get it all over with," she said. The movie was to be named *Let's Make Love*. The story was about an off-Broadway musical in which Marilyn is the star. The play is about a billionaire. Somehow, the billionaire himself goes to an audition, to see what's going on. The producers don't realize who he is, think he is an actor, and, because he looks the part, they hire him to play the billionaire. He, of course, falls in love with Marilyn, who supposedly hates rich men, and keeps up the actor impersonation to win her over.

"It's ridiculous," Marilyn said after trying to figure out the plot. "All my movies are ridiculous. At least with Fox. That's why I want to get finished, and then do exactly what I want!" Marilyn seemed remarkably eager to get in front of the cameras again. Her pregnancy situation may have also had something to do with it. During the summer she had a minor operation, which she hoped would make it possible for her to have a baby.

The operation took place at Polyclinic Hospital, where Marilyn had lost her baby the year before. Despite the terrible memories the place held for her, Marilyn had great faith in her doctor. "Going back to that hospital's a nightmare, Baby Lamb," she said, "but it's worth it for the chance of having a baby, a baby all my own." Occasionally she had talked about adopting a child, yet, to her, that would be the same as admitting defeat. Marilyn wasn't one to give up.

Marilyn had told me that the surgery was a long shot, that there was only a small chance that it would be successful. Still, the pain didn't frighten her at all. "Pain? What's pain?" she laughed nervously the day she left for the hospital. For her, the only pain was in not having her own child. I'm sure I was more worried about the actual operation than she was. "Baby Lamb, stop it," Marilyn scolded me. I couldn't help crying as she left the apartment. "You act like I'm not coming back. This isn't a big deal. Now stop crying."

She put her arms around me and kissed my cheek. "Everything's gonna be O.K. See you in a few days."

Marilyn may have been nervous in front of the cameras, as she often admitted, but when it came to things that would have terrified anyone else, no one could be braver than she was. I came down to the lobby with her to see her into the limousine with all her suitcases. It looked as if she were going on a long trip. She waved good-bye with a smile and with her fingers crossed on both hands.

I didn't see Marilyn again until the day after her surgery. She called me at her apartment, where I was doing alterations on some of the new dresses she had bought to wear that summer. When May Reis told me that Marilyn was calling, I nearly tripped as I ran to the phone. I couldn't wait to find out how Marilyn was. "Oh, I'm fine, I guess," she said. She said she wouldn't know for a while yet whether the operation had done any good. Mainly, she wanted to see me. And she was hungry. For her, the worst part of going to the hospital was hospital food. I made her some lasagna and roast chicken and hopped into a cab late that afternoon.

I found Marilyn in a small room without any view. It was very depressing, especially since there were no flowers or any other signs that Marilyn had friends who were thinking of her. There were two phones by the raised bed, but there were no books, magazines, television, or radio to help Marilyn pass the time. Yet, despite the grim atmosphere, there was Marilyn. She looked beautiful, dressed in a white satin bed jacket with maribou trim. She had bought this just for the hospital, though she had many similarly elegant night-clothes at home that she never wore. She didn't want to disappoint all the nurses and doctors, she had told me.

"Baby Lamb, my only visitor," she greeted me,

softly taking my hand in hers. Mr. Miller had been there, too, she said, "But he doesn't count. He has to come." Before I could even ask her how she was, she began digging into my food basket. She ate as if she hadn't eaten for days. "Oh, this is *so-o* good!" Her appetite told me that she would make a quick recovery.

When I told Marilyn how pretty she was, she just giggled. "I can't wait to get home and take this off. I'm on display here." Still, Marilyn seemed to have more privacy than she really wanted. I expected to see a long line of hospital workers waiting for her autograph, but, aside from the two phones, she was treated just like any other patient. "I bet they come in in a day or two," she said. "Word'll get around that I'm here." As it turned out, only one nurse and one orderly asked for Marilyn's autograph during her entire stay.

I visited the hospital each day during the week or so Marilyn was there, going by cab, bringing her food, and keeping her company. The absence of friends and flowers hadn't bothered her too much—at least, she hadn't said anything—until the day her doctor had an all-important talk with her. When I called to ask her if she wanted me to bring anything special, she told me he had been in to see her. The report wasn't what she had wanted to hear. Although the doctor had told her that she couldn't be sure about the operation until she tried to have another baby, Marilyn had gotten the impression that the surgery hadn't achieved its goal. She sounded very sad.

When I arrived at the hospital later that day, the draperies in Marilyn's room had been tightly drawn. Marilyn was lying in bed, all alone in this dark room, sobbing into her pillow. She didn't want to eat. "This place is a jinx," she wept, recalling the deep hurt she felt the last time she was here. "I just want to go home. Go home and forget. I've tried so hard, Lena. I've tried . . ."

The next day, when Marilyn left the hospital, was even worse. Last year there had been a crowd of photographers waiting for her. Now there was no one, except her limousine. I wasn't there, but Marilyn told me how dejected she felt. "Nobody cares. Nobody even knows me anymore. What good is it being Marilyn Monroe? Why can't I just be an ordinary woman? A woman who can have a family. A family? I'd settle for just one baby. My own baby. Oh, why do things have to work out so rotten?"

Marilyn was depressed for a few days, lying in bed in her room just as she had in the hospital. All things considered, though, she took things very well. She had already experienced so much heartache over the loss of her child the previous November that this blow was mild by comparison. "I'm so stupid," she said. "It's my fault. I had already given up on babies. But then there was this operation. It seemed like a ray of hope. So I got all excited again. I shouldn't have."

She tried her best to put this sadness behind her. The lack of attention at the hospital had given Marilyn something new to worry about. She felt that she had to make a new movie as soon as possible. She didn't want to be forgotten. She began spending all her time reading scripts and planning her career. "If I can't be a mother, I better be an actress. I have to be something. And, whatever it is, I'm gonna be good at it!" Marilyn's now almost daily visits to the psychiatrists and her acting classes were giving her a very positive outlook. Further, she had lost weight in the hospital, and her new, slimmer figure restored her pride in her appearance. She was as determined as I'd ever seen her.

Marilyn took such an active interest in *Let's Make Love* that she got Mr. Miller to write changes in the script that she thought would improve the movie. "We'll do it my way this time," she announced defiantly. The only difficulty with her way was that it reduced the stature of the role of the billionaire. A number of famous actors, such as Cary Grant and Rock Hudson, whom Marilyn wanted for the movie, turned it down. Gregory Peck was going to accept, but also backed out after Mr. Miller had made further alterations for Marilyn.

Now she was depressed again. "Doesn't anybody want to play with me?" she wondered aloud. Just when she began to panic that she wouldn't have a leading man, one of Mr. Miller's foreign friends came to the rescue. It was Yves Montand. Montand was in New York that fall doing a one-man song-and-dance show on Broadway. It was completely in French, but it was a big success anyway. Montand was in all the papers and was becoming a celebrity in New York. He was here with his wife, Simone Signoret, who was a major actress in France and also becoming well-known in America for her performance in the movie *Room at the Top*. She would even win an Oscar for it the next spring.

The Montands had starred several years before in a Paris production of Mr. Miller's play *The Crucible*, about the witch hunt in Salem, Massachusetts, during America's early Puritan days. Marilyn told me that when they were in England for *The Prince and the Showgirl*, Mr. Miller had gone over to Paris to see the production and had made friends with the Montands. Like Mr. Miller, they had been accused of being Communists and were given a hard time by the State Department when they wanted to visit the United States. After being rejected several times, they were

granted visas so that Mr. Montand could do his show.
Mr. Miller was eager to entertain them when they
arrived in New York.

I made a dinner for them early in their visit. I'll
never forget Marilyn's look when they came through
the door. Mr. Montand looked quite a bit like Joe
DiMaggio, and I could sense that Marilyn saw this.
Her face broke into a big smile and stayed that way all
night. It turned out that Yves was actually not French,
but Italian. He was born near Florence. He was tall,
with a big head, big mouth, big nose, yet he still
seemed quite handsome. Also, he had a special charm.
I could tell that when Marilyn introduced him to me.
He took my hand warmly, spoke in Italian, and smiled
at me in a way that made me feel as if I were the only
woman in the room—in the world—for a moment.

Yves and Simone Signoret made a strange couple.
She was obviously older than he and wasn't glamorous
at all. She wore almost no makeup, had short blonde
hair and a stocky build. Nonetheless, she looked very
intelligent. She and Mr. Miller immediately got involved in a conversation about politics. Because Mr.
Miller and Marilyn usually had so little to say to each
other, I wasn't used to hearing him talk so much.

Yves could hardly speak English, so Miss Signoret
would do a lot of translating for him. Mr. Miller tried a
few words of French himself. Marilyn barely spoke at
all. She just stared at Yves and smiled, and he kept
smiling back. They were communicating in their own
way. The four ate, drank, and had such a good time
that I couldn't understand why the Millers didn't have
guests up more often. That would have meant a lot to
Marilyn.

After they left, Marilyn couldn't wait to talk to me.
"Doesn't he look like Joe?" was the first thing she
said. "I love his voice. He's so sexy. Wow!" Marilyn

was also impressed with Simone Signoret. "Gosh, she's smart. How can he keep up with her? Oh, I guess he can, when they're speaking French. I'm going to learn French," she laughed. "It sounds like more fun than English." She said she couldn't wait to see his show.

The next day, Marilyn was on the phone for hours, asking everyone she knew everything they knew about Yves Montand. The question she kept asking was how did he end up marrying Simone Signoret. "But she's not pretty," Marilyn would say. "And she's older than he is. What did she do to get him?" Through her calls, Marilyn found out that Yves had gotten his big break as a cabaret performer because of a love affair with the great singer Edith Piaf. She was also older and not beautiful. Through Edith Piaf, Yves became a real singing star in France. She also helped him get into movies. "I bet he married Simone Signoret so she'd help him become a *big* movie star," Marilyn said. "That had to be it. For his career." Then she paused. "Well, I can't blame him. I mean, it's so hard in movies. You've gotta have connections. Anyway, she's really nice. I can tell he looks up to her. She's lucky."

Marilyn's fascination with Yves Montand increased after she saw his show. "You should see him, Lena. He's great. Imagine, if Joe could sing. That's what he'd be like." She danced a soft-shoe around her bedroom, singing "C'est Si Bon," trying to imitate Montand's suave French delivery of these three words and humming the rest. She wished aloud that she could do a movie with him. "If he would only learn English, he'd be perfect."

Marilyn kept talking about Yves to anyone who would listen. She raved about him to Mr. Miller's children and to his parents when they came to visit.

The older Millers liked him, too. They said proudly that they believed the Montands were Jewish. They knew Simone Signoret's father was Jewish and they thought Yves was Jewish, too, because his real last name was Levy. Mr. Miller corrected them. The name was spelled Livi, though Montand had nearly gotten into trouble with the Nazis because of it. Mr. Miller also told how Montand was a Resistance fighter during the war. That made him seem even more romantic to Marilyn.

Once all the American stars began to turn down *Let's Make Love,* Marilyn decided that Yves should do it. She told Mr. Miller and her other advisers, who said his English would be an impossible problem. "He's learning real fast," Marilyn said. Yves had returned to the apartment alone several times and had told Marilyn about his poor childhood—how his father worked in a factory, how he himself had to quit school at eleven to get a job, how he worked in a spaghetti factory and as a hairdresser, how he got started singing in rough Marseilles cafés, doing songs of Maurice Chevalier and imitations of Donald Duck. Marilyn was entranced. They had both come up the hard way. They had a lot in common.

Mr. Miller was usually around when Yves was there and would sometimes help translate for him and Marilyn. He seemed to trust Yves entirely. Frequently, he would return to his study to write while the other two drank champagne and chatted away while sitting on the couch next to each other. Sometimes Marilyn and Yves would hold hands while they talked, but they always let go whenever they heard the study door open. It was so cute, like two schoolchildren in love who don't want their parents to know.

Marilyn spent days on the phone pushing for Yves. She was aided by the fantastic reception his show had gotten. It was held over for weeks in New York. When he took it to Los Angeles, the film tycoons were equally impressed. For once, they agreed with Marilyn's good taste. Montand would get the role. He would learn the sound of the words, even if he didn't know what they meant. Marilyn told me that the Strasbergs tried to talk her out of Yves. "They asked me how he could understand the character if he didn't understand what he was saying. They say the part's for an older guy, somebody like Cary Grant." Yves to them simply did not seem believable as a billionaire. Marilyn didn't care. Working with him meant more to her than the movie itself. He made her happy.

As soon as Marilyn learned that Yves had the part, she began rehearsing her song-and-dance numbers with an intense determination. She'd stay up half the night struggling to learn the words of the songs. She even hired a dance teacher, a beautiful, slender girl named Mara Lynn (Marilyn often joked about the name), to teach her the routines. Not having danced since *Gentlemen Prefer Blondes,* Marilyn was a little rusty at first. She would use the living room as her stage and sometimes trip over tables or run into the sofa and bruise her legs. Practice made perfect, though.

She would put on a black leotard and black net stockings and eagerly await Mara Lynn's arrival in the afternoon. Then she would sing and dance with her around the living room for hours, until she got things exactly right. For a while, the apartment was like living on Broadway. All we needed was a big orchestra. Poor Mr. Miller looked exhausted; he stayed locked up in his study or took his dog on long walks to get away from it all. Marilyn kept working harder and harder. She had more than her fans to please this time. She had Yves.

Aside from Yves, the most exciting thing that happened to Marilyn in the months before she started *Let's Make Love* was meeting Premier Khrushchev of Russia, who was coming to visit Hollywood. This was a publicity stunt dreamed up by Twentieth Century-Fox. At first, Marilyn, who never read the papers, or listened to the news, had to be told who Khrushchev was. "Oh," she said, still unimpressed. However, the studio kept insisting. They told Marilyn that in Russia, America meant two things, Coca-Cola and Marilyn Monroe. She loved hearing that and agreed to go.

At the last minute, it was decided that Mr. Miller shouldn't go to Hollywood with her, because of all the negative publicity he had received for his allegedly left-wing views. His meeting the leading spokesman of Communism might look suspicious. He didn't seem to care. Marilyn flew out without him. She told me that the studio wanted her to wear the tightest, sexiest dress she had for the premier. The film executives also were taking him to the set of *Can-Can,* which was a risqué movie in those days. "I guess there's not much sex in Russia," Marilyn laughed.

Marilyn's main memory of Khrushchev was that he was "fat and ugly and had warts on his face and he growled." She couldn't figure out how he got to be the leader of all those people. "Who would want to be a Communist with a president like that!" she joked, and added, "I could tell Khrushchev liked me. He smiled more when he was introduced to me than for anybody else at the whole banquet. And everybody else was there. He squeezed my hand so long and so hard that I thought he would break it. I guess it was better than having to kiss him."

In the early part of 1960, Marilyn went back to Hollywood, this time with Mr. Miller, to make the movie *Let's Make Love*. They stayed, as usual, at the Beverly Hills Hotel. Excitedly, Marilyn called to tell me that in the suite directly next door were Yves and Simone Signoret. As the shooting went on, Marilyn told me she enjoyed making this picture more than any other she had done. In truth, it was the first time she really enjoyed making a movie. "It's Yves. He goes with me every morning to the studio. We come back together. We work on the script together. It's fun." Paula Strasberg was with her, too, but Marilyn really didn't need her now. "Yves is a great actor. He understands me. He's wonderful to work with. I'm not nervous anymore."

Their relationship grew even closer when Mr. Miller left for a few weeks to go to Ireland. He was going to visit the director John Huston to work together on the screenplay for *The Misfits*, which would be Marilyn's next movie. I asked her if she was going to be lonesome all by herself. "All by myself? Are you kidding? I've got Yves and Simone right next door. They'd never let me be lonesome."

Then Simone won the Academy Award as Best Actress and Yves sang at the ceremonies. She and Yves became, for the moment, the most popular couple in Hollywood. One night when Marilyn called, she couldn't conceal her envy. "She's got the Oscar. She's got Yves. She's smart. They respect her. She's got everything. What have I got?"

"You're you!" I tried to assure her. "You're the most beautiful girl in the world. Look at her and look at you. You're the one who's famous. You're the biggest star, even in France, I bet. People love you."

"Shit!" was all Marilyn could say. I knew that she wanted to win an Oscar so badly. Just to have been nominated would have been an honor for her. I had

seen how proud the Italian award had made her. At
that point, she would have sacrificed her beauty and
traded places with Simone in a second.

Then Simone had to return to Europe to begin
production on a new film. Mr. Miller had come back to
Hollywood, but he, too, decided to leave. He wanted
to spend some time with Bobby and Jane, who were
getting out of school for the summer. Marilyn would be
alone with Yves. If she had been dreaming about this,
her dream was coming true. She was very excited
when we talked, though she only hinted once that
anything improper might go on. "Baby Lamb, what
would happen if Yves . . . tried to do something? What
should I do?"

"That's up to you," I said. I knew she was crazy
about Montand, but I was old-fashioned when it came
to sex. My husband was the only man in my life. I
couldn't imagine anyone else. Nonetheless, I knew
that if she had an affair with Montand, it might make
her very happy. I wanted her to be happy. And
perhaps Mr. Miller's leaving her alone with Montand
was an effort to tell her something. "You might be
happy at first, but afterwards, you might be sorry.
I think he really loves his wife," I warned her.

"Oh, I'm just dreaming," Marilyn said with a
girlish giggle. "Nothing that exciting would happen to
me."

Marilyn constantly complained that in Hollywood
all she did was work. Her whole life was divided
between the studio and the hotel suite. Big parties and
fancy restaurants came very rarely. "The nicest thing
for me is sleep," she said. "Then at least I can
dream."

But something exciting did happen to Marilyn. She
told me all about it when she got back to New York
after completing *Let's Make Love*. "We did it! We did

it!'' Marilyn told me in a thrilled, high-pitched whisper the moment she came into the apartment and we locked ourselves in her bedroom. She clearly didn't want May Reis to hear. She was all smiles. Later that evening, she went into much more detail, obviously loving every bit of the retelling.

She admitted that she and Yves quickly drifted into an affair. "It was so natural, like we were made for each other. He's a man." "Tender," "sweet," and "kind" were the words she used again and again to describe him.

"But what about Mr. Miller?" I asked.

Marilyn said she wasn't sure. She felt hurt that he had left her alone in Hollywood. "I don't think I'm the woman for him," she said, without emotion. She had noticed that he seemed to enjoy himself far more with Simone Signoret. "Arthur needs an intellectual, somebody he can talk to. He needs someone like Simone." Then after a long pause, she broke into a big grin. "And Yves needs me." She crossed her fingers and wished that they could get married. "I don't think Arthur would care. But Simone . . . I don't know . . . I hope, I hope . . ."

Yves was due to fly back to France via New York in a few days. Marilyn had a rendezvous all planned for when he changed planes. She booked a room, under another name, naturally, at a hotel near Idlewild Airport. She ordered flowers and several big bottles of champagne. Marilyn even took two baths the day of his arrival, one in the morning and another that night before she left for the airport in her limousine. I'm not sure how much May Reis knew, but Marilyn brought her along just in case she encountered some unwanted publicity. "I pray that we don't run into any reporters. That would ruin things."

Everything that could go wrong did. The next day

when I came to work, I expected to find Marilyn aglow with beautiful memories. Instead, she was back to her tears. I hadn't seen her cry since she returned from Hollywood. "It's all over," she wept. "I was a fool. A stupid fool."

Marilyn was nearly hysterical when she described how all her plans were fouled up. First of all, several press agents and reporters were already at the airport, asking far too many snoopy questions. "Now the papers will get it. Everyone will know," she moaned. Second of all, Yves himself didn't want any part of going to the hotel with Marilyn. He wanted to get back to Paris and to Simone, as soon as possible.

"He tried to be nice," Marilyn sobbed. "He kissed me and all. But he said the idea of his leaving Simone was . . . ridiculous. That's what he said . . . ridiculous. He said he hoped I enjoyed myself with him and he told me what a 'nice time' he had had. Lena, I was in love and he was just having a 'nice time.' The last thing he said was that Arthur and I should come visit him and Simone in France. Wouldn't that be something . . . Why did I fall for him? Oh, why? I think it was when she got the Oscar. I was so jealous. I wanted to say, 'You've got the Oscar, but I've got Yves.' Now you know they're gonna be sitting in Paris and laughing their heads off at me."

Marilyn didn't have long to stay in New York. She had to leave for Nevada to begin filming Mr. Miller's film *The Misfits*. She was in no mood, though, to go anywhere. Marilyn just lay in bed, eating everything that I could prepare, listening to Frank's records, and staring at Joe's picture harder than ever. "He'd never do that to me," she said bitterly.

I tried to explain to Marilyn that European men tend to take their affairs much more casually than Americans. "Here today, gone tomorrow," I told her.

"Nobody—neither the man nor the woman—is supposed to expect anything but a good time, some good memories. That's all."

"Yeah," Marilyn sneered. "My problem was I did expect something. And look what I got! Shit, shit, shit!"

Just as Marilyn blotted *Some Like It Hot* from her memory, she likewise didn't speak again of Yves or of *Let's Make Love*. Except once. A year later, when she and Mr. Miller were divorced and Marilyn was all alone, she put on her black wig, a scarf, and dark glasses and she took me to see the movie. Unlike *Some Like It Hot*, this time we were nearly all alone in the theater one afternoon. Marilyn got a kick out of watching herself sing and dance. She did a great job on numbers like "My Heart Belongs to Daddy," and she knew it. But at the end, when she marries Yves Montand, her hands went up to her face again. This time, however, she wasn't grimacing at her appearance. She was crying, quietly but deeply, over what might have been.

Between the lasagna, hamburgers, and chocolate pudding, Marilyn was getting fat all over again. "I don't care," she snapped, when I told her how proud she had been to be thin. "Who do I need to look good for? Who?"

"Clark Gable," I replied.

She stopped eating. She was dissatisfied with many things about her next film, but starring with Clark Gable was a fantasy of hers that dated back to her childhood, when she would pretend he was her long-lost father. Actually, it was the presence of Gable and of her friend Montgomery Clift that made Marilyn go ahead with *The Misfits*. She had been complaining about the movie for many months, predicting that it was "too weird" and that it would be a failure.

The first thing she didn't like was her role, as a divorced woman who moves in with a cowboy, Clark Gable. She still hangs around with his other cowboy pals, played by Montgomery Clift and Eli Wallach (a close New York friend of the Strasbergs). The men decide to round up a herd of wild horses and sell them to be used as dog food. Marilyn, who did love animals in real life, goes along on the expedition but soon realizes how horrible this roundup is. After the men have nearly killed themselves capturing the horses, Marilyn convinces them to let the animals go free.

"I convince them by throwing a fit, not by explaining why it's wrong. I guess they thought I was too dumb to explain anything," Marilyn told me. "So I have a fit. A screaming, crazy fit. A lot worse than anything you've seen here, Lena. I mean nuts," she laughed. "And to think, *Arthur* did this to me." Marilyn blamed Mr. Miller for all she didn't like about the movie. "He was supposed to be writing this for me. He could have written me *anything* and he comes up with *this*. If that's what he thinks of me, well, then I'm not for him and he's not for me," she declared.

Another feature of the movie she resented was that is was in black and white. Again she held Mr. Miller responsible. "Arthur knew how I feel about color. I'm gonna look awful." She had been told that color would destroy the mood of the picture. "Gee, it's depressing enough as it is. Who would pay to see that? You would think with all the money they're paying for the stars and all, they'd make it in color. Then, at least, it'd look pretty. They're so stupid. Nobody would be in this movie, nobody, if it wasn't for the money." She said that Clark Gable was getting almost three quarters of a million dollars for it. She and Mr. Miller together were getting half a million. The director, John Huston, was getting over a quarter of a million dollars. "You'd think they could afford color," Marilyn said. She was sounding sarcastic, which was most unusual for her. "I'm sick of trusting people."

One of Marilyn's last fights with Mr. Miller, and probably their worst, took place during this time between movies. One afternoon, she came back into the bedroom screaming, and threw a champagne bottle against the wall, smashing it into a million slivers. "He said it's *his* movie. I don't think he even wants me in it," she barked, slamming the closet door open and shut. I thought she was going to break it off.

What Mr. Miller seemed to have told Marilyn was that his nerves, too, were starting to go. He couldn't deal with her lateness anymore. He couldn't stand Paula Strasberg's constant presence on the set. He couldn't keep embarrassing himself by having to apologize for Marilyn's problems, having to make excuses for her constantly. "He said unless I can be a 'professional'—hah—maybe I shouldn't go ahead with this." Mr. Miller had worked day and night for two years on *The Misfits*. He didn't want Marilyn to "foul it up."

Despite the fact that Marilyn had taken a risk with Yves Montand in hopes of marrying him, she couldn't believe that Mr. Miller would ever criticize her. And no matter how angry she was, she would never bring up the subject of Yves Montand and taunt Mr. Miller with her affair, even though he must have been suspicious after the airport incident was reported in the papers. She had felt guilty about it underneath and worried about hurting him. Likewise, she believed that he'd never hurt her, but now she lost her faith. "How can he say that? I'm his wife." She stormed through the living room and began pounding on the study door, which was locked. Mr. Miller refused to come out. "I'm your wife. I'm your wife," Marilyn kept screaming.

"It's not *your* movie, it's *ours*. You wrote it, but you said you wrote it for *me*. Now you say it's all yours. You lied. You lied." There was still no answer from Mr. Miller.

Marilyn kicked over some tables, banged down the keys of the piano, and grabbed another champagne bottle from the kitchen. When she returned to her room, I heard a terrible crash. She had thrown the bottle against the mirror behind her bed. Her sheets were covered with glass, and she kept slamming her body against the closet door. I grabbed her and held her tight for the longest while so she wouldn't hurt herself. Mr. Miller did not sleep in the apartment that night or any other night before they left for Nevada.

Marilyn was extremely reluctant to fly to Reno and leave the apartment. Still depressed over Yves Montand and her last fight with Mr. Miller, she spent all day either sleeping or eating. The day she left she devoured a giant bowl of spaghetti and three veal cutlets. "I'm gonna starve out there, Baby Lamb."

Marilyn begged me to come with her to Reno. "I won't be able to take it by myself. I need you to keep my spirits up. Please, please, won't you come? Just for a while?" It was very painful for me to have to say no. While I worked for Marilyn, I had felt guilty about being less than a full-time mother to my boys. I was lucky to have a family to help. But at least I could make Joey and Johnny breakfast, take them to and from school, have them with me at Marilyn's in the afternoons, and tuck them in at night. If I went to Nevada, they wouldn't have a mother at all.

Marilyn was so desperate for me to come West that she tried to arrange for me to bring the boys. She would have a private tutor for them. That was how child stars like Shirley Temple went to school, she said. The very idea of having Joey and Johnny, whom

Marilyn called "my babies," excited her tremendously. She wanted to show them off to everyone on the set. I knew that she would spend far more time on them than on her lines, but Marilyn loved the boys so much, she didn't care. She even promised that we could appear in the movie's crowd scenes. "It could be your big break," she laughed. Suddenly she began to cry. "Another dream. It won't work out. Oh, Baby Lamb, it'll be impossible without you."

I felt so sorry for her that I was almost ready to take the boys out of school and go. In a sense, Marilyn was family, too, and she seemed to need me as much as my boys did. Then my husband fell on his job and badly injured his back. He was home from work and barely able to move around. Marilyn realized that he needed me most of all. Where her friends were concerned, she could never be selfish. She insisted that I stay with him. "Your Joe comes first. I'm just going to have to be as strong as I can, Baby Lamb. But I'm going to call you . . . a lot. If I can't see you, at least I know you'll be there to listen."

When she arrived in Reno, she immediately started calling me every night just as she had promised. She needed someone to relate all her miseries to. It was too hot in Nevada. The food was awful. John Huston talked down to her. She couldn't sleep in the suite she had to share with Mr. Miller. "It's all over," she told me. "We have to stay together, 'cause it would be bad for the picture if we broke up now. It's torture. I don't know how long I can stand it. I wish I was home."

Marilyn had previously spoken highly of Huston. He had directed her in her first "big break," *The Asphalt Jungle*. "That was with Johnny [Hyde]." She felt that Huston had to be nice to her then, because of her friendship with the famous agent who was looking

out for her. Now she felt that Huston and Arthur
Miller had become close friends, especially after Mr.
Miller's trip alone to Ireland earlier that year. She
suspected they were ganging up on her. "I bet Arthur
complains to him about everything he thinks is wrong
with me. That I'm crazy, and all. That's why he
[Huston] treats me like I'm an idiot. 'Honey, this' and
'Honey, that.' Why can't he treat me like a normal
actress?" She also was annoyed that Huston seemed
to be spending all his spare time gambling in the Reno
casinos. "That's what he really likes. Not directing. I
wish he'd give me as much attention as the damn slot
machines." First, she had felt betrayed by Billy
Wilder. Now John Huston was destroying her illusions
just as harshly. Marilyn relied on having the best
directors, but the best directors were letting her down.
She felt desperate.

Marilyn was getting so upset that, in addition to
Paula Strasberg, May Reis was called out to be with
her. Marilyn also had two hairdressers, two makeup
people, a wardrobe person, a chauffeur, even a man to
give her massages—in short, an entire staff, all her
own. Even without me, she was far from alone. Yet,
she still was lonely and miserable. If Joe had been
well, Joey, Johnny, and I might have gone out to her
on the next plane.

As it was, I stayed in New York, going by the
apartment each day for a few hours, dusting, getting
the mail, doing alterations on her wardrobe (I knew
everything would have to be let out again, the way
Marilyn was eating). "Keep everything all ready for
me, Lena," Marilyn told me each night on the phone.
"I may be home any day." It was nothing for Marilyn
to jump on a plane and fly home for a weekend. She
loved flying, that is, as long as it was TWA. Somehow,
she felt superstitious about airplanes. I remember her

getting very nervous about flying after Elizabeth Taylor's husband, Mike Todd, was killed in a plane crash. "I don't know how they stay up," she said. "I've always been lucky on TWA, so I'll stick with them."

I kept waiting for Marilyn to come home. Instead, I was shocked when she called me from a hospital in Los Angeles. "It was too much. I had to come here to rest." Not only was the movie taking its toll, bad memories were also at work. The columnist Hedda Hopper wrote that Yves Montand had ridiculed Marilyn's feeling for him as a "schoolgirl crush." "It was bad enough to love me and leave me," Marilyn half-laughed, "but to kiss and tell. Some friend." Marilyn went into a tirade against gossip columnists, reporters, the whole press. "Their lives must be so dull that they have to make all this up." True or false, Marilyn was still hurt by the fact that she and Yves were being dragged into the public eye.

At one point, the producers weren't sure Marilyn could or would finish *The Misfits*. When Mr. Miller came to visit her in the hospital, she told me he was visiting not as a husband but as a spy for John Huston. "They don't want anything to happen to their precious movie," she sneered. "They probably want me to drop out so they can get Elizabeth Taylor for a million dollars." The sarcasm was growing stronger and stronger each day. Her attitude changed altogether when she got a visit from the man she needed most, Joe DiMaggio. "He came! He came! Lena, he looked so good. When you get sick, you see who really cares."

After Joe's visit, Marilyn recovered quickly and visited Joe in San Francisco on her way back to Reno. "I'm going to finish the film in no time," she told me. "Now [referring to Joe] I've something to look for-

ward to." But as soon as she reached the set and
moved back into Mr. Miller's quarters, the depression
began again. Because she felt so alone on the set,
Marilyn just couldn't relax. And she couldn't sleep.
Champagne alone would not put her out, so she re-
sorted to sleeping pills. She said she was supposed to
get up at five in the morning. However, by forcing
herself up at that hour she was useless all day. Her
only alternative was to sleep late and keep everyone
waiting. "Better late than never," she joked lamely.

Basically, Marilyn felt she had nothing to gain from
The Misfits. Mr. Miller was finished, so a desire to
please him didn't affect her. She didn't like the movie
itself and was sure her fans wouldn't. Try as she
would, she thought her role was a rotten part she could
not overcome by the best acting in the world. There
was the money, but it still wasn't as much as Elizabeth
Taylor got; whatever it was, it wasn't enough. All that
kept her going, then, were the two stars: Gable and
Clift.

That she bothered to get up at all is more a tribute
to Clark Gable than to Marilyn's sense of duty. She
loved being around him; she wanted him to like her.
She felt he did. "He never got angry with me once, for
blowing a line or being late, or anything. He never
raised his voice, lost his temper. Not like Tony Curtis.
He was a gentleman, the best." Marilyn described to
me her most exciting scene with Gable. Marilyn was in
the bedroom the morning after she and Gable had
spent their first night together. Gable comes in and
finds her wrapped only in a sheet (which is how
Marilyn slept in real life). The scene was shot several
times, with Gable kissing her good morning. On one
take, Marilyn told me, she was so electrified by
Gable's kisses that she let the sheets drop and he acci-
dentally placed his hand on one of her breasts. "I got

goose bumps all over," Marilyn exclaimed. "That kiss . . . that touch . . . oh!"

"What was it like?" I pressed anxiously.

"It was like . . . like . . . Clark Gable. What more can I say? Just like in the movies, when I saw him as a little girl and I dreamt about kissing him. And I did it! I did it!" She was in paradise.

Marilyn told me she slept perfectly that night, without one pill. She dreamt about doing even more with Gable. "But that was a dream. He treated me like I was his little girl. Sometimes he'd pinch me and say, 'Get to work, beautiful' or 'Why are sexy women so late?' Other times, he'd give me a little squeeze on my ass and call me 'chubby' or 'fatso.' I always wanted to reach out and throw my arms around him and kiss, kiss, kiss him, but I was too scared. I mean, you just can't go up and kiss Clark Gable. But once, after a really good scene, he kissed me on the lips and said, 'Thanks.' I'll never forget it."

Marilyn said that she couldn't conceal her lifelong admiration for "The King," as Gable was known in Hollywood. "You wouldn't believe how modest he was. He always said, 'There's a million guys look better than me.' One story he liked to tell on the set was that whenever some of his women fans tracked him down, telling him how handsome he was, he'd just pull out his false teeth to show that 'I'm an old man, just like all the rest.'" Marilyn couldn't have cared. She saw Gable as a father figure, if not her father himself. She gave her best for him and him alone. Having Gable as her leading man was an honor she would always treasure.

If Gable represented Marilyn's father, Marilyn saw Montgomery Clift as her son, or maybe her baby brother. "If they think I've got troubles, they should look at Monty. He's more messed up than anybody,"

she would say. Clift, who was one of Hollywood's best
and best-looking young actors, had been horribly
disfigured in an automobile wreck. Marilyn said he
never got over it. He drank and took drugs all the time.
Marilyn felt very protective toward him. He was the
only big name in the cast that was on Marilyn's
"side," as she described her conflict with Mr. Miller.
(Huston, Eli Wallach, and all the assistant directors,
cameramen, etc., were all on "Arthur's side." Clark
Gable seemed to be above all of this.) "With all that
stuff about me and Yves in the papers, no wonder they
all feel sorry for Arthur. It makes me look like a tramp.
And Arthur looks so pitiful, too; God, I don't blame
them for hating me. I know he'd never hurt me—he'd
do anything. But we're wrong, the two of us—this
marriage is all wrong. And it's impossible to explain it
to the others here. It's none of their damn business. So
they keep thinking it's all my fault, that I'm a mean
bitch. I'm not, Lena, you know I'm not."

Marilyn called me, in tears, one day when Clift was
injured during a rodeo scene. "He's so frail and sick,
Lena. I hope he'll be all right . . . fast. He's the only
friend, the only star friend I've got. If he's out sick, I
won't have anybody. I'm so scared." Luckily Clift
recovered and was good company for Marilyn. "We
try to figure out for each other what to do and take to
fall asleep. He can't sleep either," she said. "Monty's
just like me."

Marilyn was terrified that Mr. Miller and John
Huston would rewrite her scenes to make her seem
even crazier. "It's their movie. It's really about the
cowboys and the horses. That's all they need. They
don't need me at all. Not to act. Just for the money. To
put my name on the marquee. To trick the people into
paying to see another dumb blonde sex movie. Well,
they'll be sorry on this one."

After she got out of the Los Angeles hospital, Marilyn did come home for several weekends, before returning to New York for good in early November 1960. "Home, sweet home" she'd always shout as she burst through the door, giving me a long hug and a kiss. She would immediately dash into her bedroom, take off her clothes, get under the covers, and ask me for champagne and some Italian specialty she liked. "This is the only place I can sleep. I'm so glad. I can have my own bed now. And good food. At last." Marilyn looked terrible, huge bags under her eyes, pale, too heavy, jittery. She kept talking about all the pressure of the film, both with the director and with Mr. Miller, who had not returned with her. "He's gone," she said simply, with neither a smile nor a frown. "It's our house now, Baby Lamb, just me and you." She pulled me over and gave me another kiss. "Oh, Lena, I'm so happy to be home."

8

The period of relaxation Marilyn was looking forward to after *The Misfits* didn't last long at all. First, she was besieged with phone calls about her separation from Mr. Miller. Yes, it was true, she told them. One day Mr. Miller came to get his typewriter, books, and papers from the study. Marilyn stayed locked in her room. Mr. Miller didn't say a word to her or to me. He looked very sad, as if he might cry at any moment. "Tell me when he's gone," Marilyn whispered.

The moment he closed the door, with the last load of his possessions, Marilyn took me with her to the study and cautiously opened the door that had remained closed nearly the entire time she had been in the apartment. Aside from the desk, chair, and bookcases, the room was bare. It looked so depressing. The only sign of life was a photo of Marilyn. She seemed hurt that he had left it behind. "He really wants to forget," she said, as a little tear trickled down her cheek. "I guess I'm gonna have to forget, too. Come on, Baby Lamb, please drink some champagne with me. Please. I need a friend."

The loneliness Marilyn felt at Mr. Miller's silent departure was underscored by the sudden death of Clark Gable a few days later. Gable had had a severe heart attack the very day after they finished *The Misfits*. Everyone thought he would recover and he seemed to be making excellent progress. Then he died. Marilyn was in shock. She had really grown to love Gable on the movie and had talked to me about making another film with him when he got better.

"I loved him, Lena. He was so nice to me. He was always smiling, always encouraging. If anyone in the world could have looked down on me, it was him. He was the biggest star of all. But he respected me. I just saw him. He kissed me good-bye. My friend . . . Oh, God, why is he dead?"

As upsetting to Marilyn as Clark Gable's death were the vicious rumors that she killed him. He had a weak heart before production started. Marilyn's lateness and her fights with Arthur Miller were said to have caused a terrible tension Gable kept to himself, because he was such a gentleman. All the bottled-up pressure was too much, the Hollywood gossip went. This filtered through to Marilyn over phone calls and in the papers she made May Reis let her read.

"That's horrible," Marilyn said, her face white with fear at the mere suggestion that she was at fault. "He couldn't have just pretended he liked me . . . could he? Wouldn't he have said something if he was mad? Everyone else did. All he had to do was tell me. I would have been up at five o'clock. No matter what. I'd have done anything." She started to sob hysterically. "Oh, I did. I did it. I was so selfish. Oh, Jesus, I did. I killed him. God forgive me. Oh, no!"

Marilyn had been tormented like this when she had recalled the death of her friend Johnny Hyde. She felt she could have saved him by marrying him. Now she became convinced that she could have saved Clark Gable by being on time. I tried my hardest to convince her that it wasn't her fault, that she had meant no one any harm. Marilyn literally wouldn't have hurt a fly. She was so gentle, so sad. But somehow she got it into her head that she was responsible for Gable's heart attack. The awful nightmares started, then it became impossible for her to sleep without ever-increasing doses of sleeping pills. She even lost her appetite. For days, she would lie on the bed, her eyes bulging out, wringing her hands in frustration.

One afternoon, in December 1960, she decided to go out shopping. It seemed like a good idea, to get her mind off her troubles. It wasn't. New York was aglow with the Christmas season. All the stores were decorated gaily. People were buying gifts for friends and family. Lovers were strolling down Fifth Avenue, taking in all the sights. And Marilyn was all alone. She came back to the apartment, empty-handed and crying. There was no tree, no gifts, no cards. The place was cold and lonely. I felt sorrier for her than ever.

I made Marilyn a big Italian dinner to cheer her up. When I returned to her room, she hadn't eaten a thing. She just stared at the food. "Take it away, please," she said. About seven thirty, I came back to see how she was. Something told me that I had better watch her closely. My instincts were correct. The curtains to one of the bedroom windows had been pulled apart, which was almost never done, for Marilyn liked it dark. Furthermore, the window was wide open. Marilyn was standing before it with her white robe on. She normally never wore anything in the bedroom, except when there were guests. The only time she even came near the window was to wave good night to me. This was more than strange. Both of her hands grasped the outside molding. It looked as if she might jump.

I ran over and surprised Marilyn by grabbing her around the waist. She turned around and fell into my arms. "Lena, no. Let me die. I want to die. I deserve to die. What have I got to live for?"

"Are you crazy?" I said, closing the window and curtains. "What's the matter with you?"

"I can't live anymore. What have I done with my life? Who do I have? It's Christmas! I want to have a Christmas. I never had one . . . I never will."

"You'll have a Christmas. A nice one. And lots of them, I promise."

"Baby Lamb." Marilyn hugged me for a long time, until she stopped shivering.

I told her that now she should call Joe DiMaggio. That would cheer her up. She agreed, and dialed his number. After finally reaching him, she chatted for nearly an hour. I came back in to find her smiling through her tears. "Gee, how could I have been so crazy? I just lost control for a second. I didn't know what I was doing."

I teased her for wearing her robe when she planned to jump. "The suicide was going to be the most modest thing you ever did around here." She started laughing.

"I thought about dressing up. I did . . . really. But my hair's a mess anyway, so I figured, what the hell? Hey, why *did* I put the robe on? Crazy . . . gee, I'm sorry." Marilyn was now feeling well enough that I was able to feed her. Afterward, she took a sleeping pill and fell fast asleep. I called my husband and told him I wouldn't be home that night. She was going to be all right, but I didn't want to take any chances.

I had been through this sort of thing once before with Marilyn about a year earlier. Mr. Miller had been away in Connecticut, and Marilyn had gone out to dinner with some people visiting from Hollywood. She had given me the night off. When I arrived the next morning at eight, I found her unconscious on her bedroom rug, her face caked with the remains of her dinner, which she had thrown up next to her. Unable to wake her, I called the doctor, whose number was posted on an Emergencies list in May Reis's office.

The doctor, a fat, friendly man, came immediately, pumped Marilyn's stomach, and put her in bed. When May arrived, she called Mr. Miller in from Connecticut. He rushed back, very concerned. Once Marilyn was awake, she smiled weakly and asked, with all innocence, "What did I do? Oh, am I hungry." I made her some spaghetti, and, after eating it all in an instant, she told me what had happened. She had gotten all dressed up to go out (I had helped her) but found herself very depressed when no one at all noticed her at the restaurant. Also, her companions barely complimented her. They just talked business. She was so unhappy with the evening that she was unable to fall asleep. First, one sleeping pill, then two, then three, but nothing worked. "I got so mad about not dozing off, that I just gulped a whole handful. I don't know how many. That knocked me out for sure. But I didn't mean to kill myself. Jesus, I'm not that far gone. I don't want to die. I've got too much to do."

I reminded Marilyn of this story when she awoke the day after her near jump, and she agreed. "Gee, how can I die before I've made the movies I want? And I'm gonna make them, Lena. I'm gonna be strong. No more yesterdays. I promise." I was relieved to see her determination. Yesterday was a bad dream I prayed would never occur again.

Marilyn may have told May Reis about her thoughts on suicide. Whatever, May was clearly worried about Marilyn's pre-Christmas depression. They talked for hours about a will, and both May and Marilyn had long conversations on the phone with Marilyn's lawyers on the subject. "They say I need a will," Marilyn said. "They really want to finish me off," she laughed. "A will. Imagine. I thought that was something old people did. Well, if it will shut everyone up, they can have their will. Won't do anyone any good, cause I'm gonna stick around for a while." I could tell her spirits were improving. "What do you want me to leave you, Baby Lamb?"

"Nothing," I smiled. "Just don't you leave." Marilyn thought the whole thing was hilarious. When the lawyers came up to work on the will, she made a point of getting especially drunk. "This whole thing is so creepy," she said. I remember hearing her ask if she could change her will if she wanted to; the answer was yes. "I'll change it when I'm older and really need to worry about it," she told me when they left. "I just wanted to get this over with now. I got the feeling the next thing was they'd bury me. Ugh! Hey, Lena, be sure to keep these windows closed," she giggled.

Within a few days, I felt much better for Marilyn. She was making jokes, eating, listening to music. But the real reason for her recovery was that Joe DiMaggio had finally come to her. He always came late, after dinner, and left early the next morning, before May Reis arrived. He always came up the service elevator, through the kitchen door. "He doesn't want any publicity," Marilyn explained. "Zero." And he always wore a suit. He was one of the most distinguished men you could imagine. He really did inspire confidence and nobody needed it more than Marilyn. The way he kissed her hello, the calm, solid way he talked to her, the powerful arm he always draped around her—this was what she needed to pull herself together.

In addition to Joe, who frequently brought flowers, the gifts and cards also started to arrive. My little boys each carved Marilyn a fat snowman out of soap, using chunks of coal for the eyes and nose. They scribbled her a note, "To our friend, Marilyn. Love and Merry Christmas, Joe and Johnny Pepitone." That meant the world to her; she kept the snowmen by her bed. They always brought a smile. My husband sent her a card, as did several other members of my family who had met her at the apartment. With all they had heard about Marilyn from me, they felt her a part of our big family. As for myself, I had spent months knitting Marilyn a beige angora sweater. I remember her crying happily when she opened it. "See, you had a Christmas," I said.

"Oh, Lena, you've saved me. You really have." Her gift to me was an envelope overflowing with hundred-dollar bills. Marilyn wasn't one to shop for presents; whenever she gave anything, she gave cash. Of course, the money was needed, but it was Marilyn's kind thought behind it that gave her gift a special meaning for me.

When Marilyn was with Mr. Miller, New Year's Eve had been the loneliest night of the year. On December 31, 1960, Marilyn insisted I go home early to be with my family. I refused at first, reluctant to leave her alone, but she announced proudly she had "a guest" coming and that she'd be fine. I was pretty sure who "the guest" would be. At 11:15 that night, however, just as we were about to welcome in the New Year at home, the phone rang. "Baby Lamb, I hate to do this, but I was wondering if you could make us a special New Year's dish. If you're busy, that's all right . . ."

"Go! Go!" my husband insisted. "She needs you. We'll celebrate later."

What Marilyn wanted was spaghetti cooked with sweet Italian sausages. Luckily, we had plenty in the house, and off I went. The limousine was waiting for me downstairs. When I came into the kitchen, there were Marilyn and Joe, with happy, hungry smiles on their faces. They stayed in the kitchen while I cooked things up quickly. We all ate spaghetti and sausages and toasted the New Year together. Joe kissed Marilyn, then me. That alone was worth the trip. They refused to allow me to clean up; instead they sent me back home with a two-hundred-dollar tip—all for an hour's work. They were tightly in each other's arms as they waved good night. I prayed that the rest of the year would go as well for Marilyn as the beginning.

The next morning, I served Marilyn and Joe a big breakfast at the dining room table. They both were sitting on the same side, holding hands. He called her "Darling" and was affectionate in a way she hadn't known with Mr. Miller. I could see she loved him like no one else. She had on her white robe. He, always formal, had on a white shirt and tie. The picture in her closet was a dream come true. Although Marilyn's eyes were glazed from what must have been a long night, she was in heaven that New Year's Day.

When Marilyn left the table to change into some slacks, Joe and I talked Italian together as he sipped his milk. He refused coffee, as he had an ulcer he was treating. He may have been famous, but he was very sympathetic, easy to be with. So I came out with what was on my mind. "Why don't you marry Marilyn again? She loves you. It would be wonderful for her."

Joe just shook his head sadly. He said that he loved her more than any other woman, that he'd do anything for her. But marriage . . . they had too many differences that just didn't work. He felt, as always, that her career was what was killing her. If only she would forget it and stick with him, then they could be happy as man and wife. But as long as she wanted any part of Hollywood . . . Joe held his stomach, indicating a terrible pain—there was no way they could live together without fighting. Despite Joe's reluctance, I kept hoping that he might change his mind.

Marilyn kept hoping, too. She did not disguise her frustration at Joe's inflexible attitude. "He's stubborn as a mule," she despaired. Nevertheless, she was so happy just to have Joe around for the present that she tried to avoid thinking about the future. "At least he's here," she would say. "Maybe something will work out. I won't give up."

Marilyn was getting more and more optimistic, talking about trips she and Joe would take, talking about new movies. Scripts came in every day, as did phone calls about film projects. In January, she left the apartment briefly to fly to Mexico. There, in a border town, she got her divorce from Mr. Miller. When she returned, her spirits were as good as before. Then Mr. Miller's mother died unexpectedly. This was a major setback, for Marilyn loved Mrs. Miller as her own mother and spoke with her on the phone even after the separation.

Now Marilyn felt guilty about Mrs. Miller's death. "She begged me to stay with Arthur, to keep trying. I let her down, too. She was a wonderful person . . . an angel. I can't believe it." Marilyn was stunned. Added to her deep grief at the loss of her mother-in-law came the shock of further gossip about Clark Gable's death. It was reported that even Gable's wife held Marilyn responsible. She felt guilty enough and couldn't bear to be reminded.

With Joe in Florida, Marilyn had no one to lean on except her psychiatrists, to whom she had never stopped going, yet even they couldn't console her. She drank more and took more and more pills. Still, she couldn't sleep. One day when she went to see one of her psychiatrists, she didn't come back. The next morning, when I arrived to find her room empty, Pat Newcomb, a young lady assigned to Marilyn by her public relations agency, told me Marilyn had been taken to the Payne Whitney Clinic. The Payne Whitney Clinic, about ten blocks away from the apartment on the East River, was known as the "rich people's crazy house." And I knew Marilyn didn't want to be any place like that.

She evidently hated the place so much that within a couple of days she had called Joe DiMaggio in Florida to get her out. Joe flew right up and had Marilyn transferred uptown to Columbia Presbyterian Hospital. There she had a private room. With no bars. "Payne Whitney was a prison," she said, still frightened, when I came up with homemade food and robes for her to wear. "There were bars, really bars, and steel doors and padded cells. They were going to put me in a straitjacket. That place is for real nuts! Thank God for Joe! Thank God!"

Marilyn didn't want to think that she was crazy. She wasn't. She was unhappy. But it disturbed her to feel that the psychiatrist she trusted so much thought that she was crazy. Eventually, this doctor convinced Marilyn that there had been a misunderstanding. Nevertheless, with her mother in a sanitarium and her grandmother having died in one, the thought of insanity gave Marilyn something new to worry about.

In her several weeks up at Columbia, I came almost every day for a visit, and with food—soup, pastas, chocolate pudding. I had not visited Marilyn at Payne Whitney. I tried, but visitors weren't allowed there. It was so frustrating, wanting to see Marilyn and being told things like, "We don't have any such person here." The staff was so cold, so distant. I could see why Marilyn felt imprisoned there. Columbia Presbyterian was a much more pleasant place. Although I wasn't sure what the visiting rules were, I took the subway up there as soon as I found out where Marilyn was. I knew how much she hated being alone. When I finally got in to see her, she began crying, just out of happiness. "You found me. You found me, Lena!" she smiled. She was white, pale, and totally exhausted. She needed a rest, but not one that was forced on her, against her will.

The Columbia hospital was much more cheerful than Polyclinic (where she had lost her baby) had been, if only for the many bouquets of flowers that filled Marilyn's room. "Joe sent them," she said. "He's done everything for me." She told me that she was going to stay there for a couple of weeks. The doctors, she explained, were going to help her calm down and get to sleep without sleeping pills. "It'll be nice just to close my eyes and fall asleep. To forget."

Marilyn was very upset that I had taken the long subway ride uptown. She spent more time thanking me for caring about her than in talking about her night-mares and other troubles. She made sure that someone on the hospital staff got me a cab home and that I had plenty of cab fare each time I came to visit. I would only stay less than an hour, and Marilyn seemed to enjoy every minute, even if all I did was sit there watching her eat. "It's nice to have a friend," she'd say.

Each time I came, I'd bring a new nightgown for Marilyn to wear. She loved the variety. In fact, the gowns were one of the big events of her day, along with my food and the frequent visits of the hospital psychiatrists. Otherwise, Marilyn said, she spent her time doing nothing at all. "I guess that's what they mean by relaxing,'' she told me. Yet, Marilyn didn't mind this extremely quiet existence. "I miss my Frankie records,'' was her only real complaint.

At the beginning of her stay, Marilyn was getting a lot of shots to steady her nerves. These gradually grew less and less frequent. The treatment was clearly working. Every day, Marilyn looked a little stronger. The color returned to her face, and she bragged that she was getting whole nights' sleep without the help of a single pill or glass of champagne. "Not one bad dream,'' she announced triumphantly. Soon, she was able to go home. The rest, away from the ringing phone and all the rumors, had done her good. She was, nonetheless, glad to be back in her own bed and among her own possessions. One of the first things she did was to try on a dozen or more of her evening dresses, as if to make sure she still looked glamorous. She had been wearing nightgowns and robes for so long, it was fun for her to dress up. But it was more fun to take everything off. She couldn't go naked in the hospital and that annoyed her. "I'll never wear a nightgown again,'' Marilyn vowed as she stretched out nude on her bed. "I'm free,'' she boasted, "free.''

Mr. Miller had kept his dog, Hugo, but now Marilyn had a pet of her own. Frank Sinatra had given her a cute little white French poodle. "This is my baby, mine and Frankie's,'' Marilyn said, cuddling the dog in her arms. She named the poodle "Maf,'' which was short for Mafia. Marilyn always teased Frank about his Italian friends. "They all look like gangsters to me, even though they're not,'' she laughed. She thought it was a great joke to name the dog after The Mob. "Frankie couldn't stand that name. He said it was dumb to call a French poodle Mafia. 'Why not Fifi or Pierre; you know, something French?' Plus, he said it made him look bad. That was really it. He's so proper sometimes. Him and his image. But I told Frankie, 'Nothing can make you look bad,' so he let me keep the name.'' Maf became my responsibility too. Because Marilyn didn't like to go outside the apartment, I had to walk Maf several times a day.

Marilyn also had other company besides Maf. Of course, there was Joe, but his many business commitments prevented him from being around all the time. Then there was Frank, whom Marilyn would see not only in New York but on two- or three-day excursions to Los Angeles, taking Maf in her lap. She used the airplane the way we would use a car on a weekend outing. And then there was her masseur. Marilyn had decided that massages were a great way to "lose weight." Accordingly, she employed a tall, dark, good-looking man to give her massages. He wasn't muscular, the way I thought masseurs were supposed to be, though Marilyn assured me, "He has the best hands in the world."

Her massage routine was an odd one. The man would come about six in the morning and would be finishing up about the time I arrived for work. The exercise would take place on a table in Mr. Miller's old study, which had now become Marilyn's "gym." Like Mr. Miller, Marilyn began keeping the door closed. When I came in, I would hear the craziest giggling and screeching, both from Marilyn and the masseur.

I noticed that Marilyn always had taken a bath before these sessions and had drenched herself with perfume. She would emerge from the study hot, sweaty, and naked, though she never bathed afterward. She just went to bed and slept till lunchtime. Then she awoke with the biggest appetite. "If you get massages, you'll never need another sleeping pill," she laughed. "I'm so-o-o relaxed." The masseur, dressed in white, would usually have a cup of coffee in the kitchen before going home. He looked exhausted, yet he never lost his big smile.

Still another of Marilyn's male friends was her Italian chauffeur, who could have been a stand-in for Rudolph Valentino. Marilyn loved his dark costume and cap, and she referred to him as "The Sheik." She would frequently invite him up for champagne and would ask him to take her for rides, even when she had nowhere to go. The chauffeur, whose name was Johnnie, worked for the limousine service that Marilyn used. Even while she was with Mr. Miller, she always insisted that the service assign Johnnie as her driver.

After Mr. Miller left, Marilyn used the limousine service less and less. "The Sheik," however, continued his frequent visits. But now he came to see Marilyn as a friend, not an employee. Sometimes, they'd lock themselves up in her room for the whole afternoon. Marilyn would usually dress up in a tight, black cocktail dress, put on makeup for him, and have a big tray of caviar and champagne set out for his enjoyment. Again, the squealing, laughing, and other noises filled the house, but Marilyn never said anything about Johnnie to me. She just winked when he left, and I winked back.

She could sit for hours, talking about movie stars and other men she knew, rating them on their sexiness and dreaming about what it might be like to be their girlfriend. When chatting about her early Hollywood days, she told me that she would have slept with almost anybody who asked her, regardless of what their looks were. The only real requirement was that they be "nice." "If it would make them happy, why not? It didn't hurt me. I like to see men smile."

She did admit that she had preferences, though. At the top of the list were older men who she could pretend were her father. They didn't have to be handsome, "just warm and strong, like a father could be." When I asked her if she could sleep with any man in the whole world whom would she choose, she didn't hesitate a second. "Clark Gable," she said, and then started to cry. She really did love him. Who was the last person she'd ever want to sleep with? "Billy Wilder, without question. He probably feels the same way about me. If he was attracted to me, he would have treated me better."

Aside from older men, Marilyn loved strong, dark Italians. She said that she liked men who took charge, told her what to do, dominated her. "That's why Frankie and Joe are so great. They're the boss. They run the show. I'm not very aggressive, but they sure are."

I said I was surprised to hear this about Frank. Joe, of course, was a powerful athlete, but Frank was so skinny and weak-looking. "Oh, no, Lena, he's tough, real tough." Then she broke out in the naughtiest grin. "You know, Frankie and Joe have one thing in common."

"What's that?"

She covered her face with her hands and couldn't control her laughter. "I can't . . . I can't say it."

"Come on."

She was laughing so hard the tears were pouring down her cheeks. When Mr. Miller was around, Marilyn rarely would even joke about sex. Now I could see that she loved it, and was fascinated by it. Perhaps that would keep her happy.

Marilyn told me of her dreams about movie stars like Clark Gable and Tyrone Power sweeping her off her feet and making love to her in places that sounded like movie sets—rich palaces, tropical islands, yachts, sleek trains. She was unquestionably a romantic person, with fantasies of glamorous romance which Mr. Miller, locked in his study, never fulfilled.

In truth, while she gave Joe DiMaggio the highest praise as a great lover, they didn't go to any romantic spots either. And Frank, she complained, liked to go on such elegant evenings but never with her. "He always kept me in the bedroom." She talked about the Fred Astaire movies of her youth—top hat, white tie and tails, dressing up, champagne, caviar—and not all alone in her room. She wanted to do the town: "Isn't that what New York's all about? I just need the right guy to do it with." Perhaps Yves Montand was the closest Marilyn ever came to this dream of sophistication. He was debonair, European, charming, but she never mentioned him anymore. Marilyn knew how to forget certain deep hurts. It was one important way she was able to survive.

One man Marilyn thought of all the time was Montgomery Clift. She often thought that she might be in love with him, for she felt closer to him than to any other star. "He needs me. He needs someone. I'd love to help him. Oh, but he's so impossible." Monty, as she called him, would come over to the apartment to visit, usually dressed in shabby clothes that looked as if he had slept in them for days. He always had a stubble of a beard and was hunched over. The terrible wreck that he was in had made a sick old man out of a beautiful young one. "He was the best-looking guy I've ever seen. He was perfect." Marilyn would sometimes cry just thinking about Monty's bad luck. "See, Lena, you can't count on your looks. Anything can happen."

Like a concerned mother, Marilyn didn't think Monty was eating right. She'd always have me prepare a big steak for him, and, the minute he arrived, she'd

lead him to the dining room table where a feast had
been set out. He pushed everything aside. All he
wanted was caviar and straight vodka, which he drank
like water. Sometimes he'd take a pill and wash it
down with vodka. Marilyn begged him to eat, but he
simply shook his head. Seeming to be in a trance, he
just drank, stared, and mumbled to Marilyn. They
would talk about movies, sharing stories about how
terrible Hollywood was. They talked about their
psychiatrists. Now Monty was going to play one—
Freud. That amused both of them. "I wish I could play
one, too," Marilyn said. "God, you and I know more
about them than anybody." However, Marilyn warned
Monty about working again with John Huston, who
had directed them both in *The Misfits*. "He's a mean
bastard. He'll use you," she said. "Maybe it's just
with me, but I'd be careful."

They would also talk about drugs. The only time
Monty showed any enthusiasm at all was when he'd
describe some new pain-killer or sleeping pill a doctor
had recommended. Marilyn would always nag him to
write down the name. She would invariably call her
own doctor to ask about the pill the minute Monty had
left.

"He needs a woman to love him," Marilyn announced one day. "Just like I need someone." Marilyn told me the stories she had heard that Monty was a
homosexual. She didn't want to believe them at all.
The notion of a man sleeping with another man struck
Marilyn as incredibly weird. "Why would he do that?
He could have any girl in the world. . . ." Besides, she
knew Monty was good friends with Elizabeth Taylor,
whom he never discussed with Marilyn and whom
Marilyn was too proud to ask about. Nevertheless, she
kept regarding Elizabeth as her chief rival and sometimes couldn't hide her jealousy of her. The million

dollars Elizabeth was getting for *Cleopatra* continued to annoy Marilyn. Then Marilyn brought up a new way in which she was competing with Elizabeth, and losing. "I bet Monty sleeps with her. I bet he does," Marilyn declared. "Why her?"

Suddenly, Marilyn decided that if Elizabeth Taylor could sleep with Montgomery Clift, why couldn't she? She liked him more than anyone else in show business and wanted him to feel the same way about her. Seducing him became a big challenge for her. On the day he was going to come over, Marilyn had her hair and nails done and picked out a very sexy outfit. Normally, all she wore was her white robe, and looked as sloppy as Monty. Today would be different.

Marilyn selected a pair of white pants with a matching while silk blouse. Both were skintight and revealed every contour of her body. She even wore matching white high heels, and drenched herself with Joy, on her arms, behind her knees, her thighs, her stomach. She gulped champagne to calm her nerves. Monty did a slight double take when he walked through the door. "You've got company," he apologized, thinking he had come on the wrong day.

"Only you," Marilyn whispered softly. Monty seemed confused. Instead of sitting at the dining room table, Marilyn lured Monty to the couch, where she fed him caviar with a spoon. She was sitting nearly on top of him, but he didn't make a move, not even when she sighed and lay down on the couch with her head in his lap. He just kept drinking and mumbling occasionally, as usual. Because Marilyn was so shy, this was absolutely as far as she could go. She told me later that she didn't have the nerve to reach up and kiss him.

Realizing that the couch was a dead end, Marilyn soon got up to pour some champagne. Then, holding her glass, she walked back and forth in front of Monty, who was still slouching on the sofa. Her steps were very self-conscious, her hips swaying in the most alluring way. The light streaming through the windows was certainly to her advantage, showing off her spectacular figure. As I came in with a caviar refill, Marilyn gave me a hopeless shrug. Then, without notice, Monty stood up and walked over to Marilyn. I watched from the hallway, hoping that she had accomplished her purpose. Her big smile told me she thought the same.

But instead of sweeping Marilyn into his arms, Monty pulled back his hand to give her a teasing swat on her backside. "You've got the most incredible ass," he said, and pecked her cheek. "Listen, I've got to go. See you." As he closed the door behind him, Marilyn fell back on the couch and started giggling.

"I give up, Lena. I tried. Boy, I tried. You know, I kinda doubt that he does anything with Elizabeth Taylor, either. I think I was wrong about that. He's a mess. . . . I still love him."

All in all, it was a great effort, against losing odds. Marilyn didn't take it personally. She had a lot of fun trying. She went back to her bedroom and stripped off her clothes. Then she put on a Sinatra record, lay on the bed, and daydreamed away the rest of the afternoon.

9

If Marilyn was taking a new interest in sex, she was definitely losing interest in becoming a "serious dramatic actress." Not only did she see less of the Strasbergs, she also began to question their enthusiasm in encouraging her to depart from the "dumb blonde" roles that had made her famous. Having been away from moviemaking for many months, Marilyn now began to enjoy her fame more than ever and was eager to get back into the public eye. "It's better for the whole world to know you, even as a sex star, than never to be known at all," she said. "If I'm that famous [as her press agents assured her daily that she was], I'll get the good parts soon enough. I'm not going to kill myself by trying to rush it."

After all, *The Misfits* was as serious a movie as they come. Yet, despite the stars and all the talent that went into the movie, it was doing badly at the box office. Nor were the reviews that wonderful. *Let's Make*

Love wasn't doing that well either. On the other hand, *Some Like It Hot* was a smash, not only in America but all over the world. Marilyn didn't like to admit it, yet this was the kind of movie that audiences wanted her in. Nobody wanted to see Marilyn scream and cry as in *The Misfits*. They wanted to see her laugh, and to laugh with her. She had a special gift to make people happy. She realized that, at least for the time being, she should stick with it.

Even though she struck out with Monty Clift, Marilyn began to be impressed with the idea that she was Hollywood's "Queen of Sex." She kept on her diet, took better care of her hair and skin, and never stopped looking in the mirror. "I look pretty good for an old lady in her thirties, don't I, Lena?" she would ask me constantly, while strutting nude before her mirrors. She did, indeed.

Marilyn even began sending down for copies of *Playboy* magazine. She'd open the foldout, of some girl in her late teens or early twenties, look at it, then look at herself. "I'm better," she'd say. "Hmm . . . not bad, even if I have to say so. . . . What do you think?" She always needed encouragement. Sometimes she would talk about appearing in *Playboy*. She was worried that she had been out of sight for too long and about the bad publicity her hospital stays might have gotten her. "If I were in *Playboy,* that would sure make everyone know I'm still around."

Marilyn's growing self-confidence did suffer a serious setback in the summer of 1961. For a long time she had been having problems with her digestion. I had thought all her burping came from the champagne bubbles. Instead, it was her gall bladder. She went into surgery to have it removed. Although the operation was a success, the scar on the right side of her stomach seemed to shatter her whole view of herself. Her white, creamy skin had never had a blemish before, and now here was this nasty-looking gash.

In addition to the scar, Marilyn began to see a lot of other things she had never noticed before. First, her breasts. Before she used to poke her chest out and take pride in how firm they were. Now she decided that they were getting flabby. She discovered tiny stretch marks there and on her backside, probably from the gaining and losing of so much weight. Her face was beginning to show an occasional line. "I'm getting crow's-feet," she gasped. For the first time, Marilyn could sense that she was growing older. It terrified her.

"I don't want to get old, Baby Lamb. I want to stay like I am. I still can't act . . . not really. Monty had his looks, but when he lost them, he was still a great actor. I'm not. I won't fool myself anymore. When my face goes, my body goes, I'll be nothing . . . nothing . . . all over again." She broke down sobbing.

Aside from the operation, her high spirits were dampened when several projects she wanted fell through. The first was a television production of *Rain*, the Somerset Maugham story of Sadie Thompson, the Pago Pago prostitute, gold teeth and all. A year before, if Marilyn had been asked to play a prostitute, she would have been insulted. Now she was flattered. Even though she wasn't playing Queen Victoria, as she might have insisted on earlier, Lee Strasberg gave his approval for the part. If he says so, Marilyn thought, it must be O.K. Unfortunately, the television network did not give its approval to Lee as the director. They said that he had no TV experience; they preferred to use one of their own directors.

Marilyn was completely loyal to her friends. She said, "It's Lee or nothing." The result was nothing, with Marilyn sacrificing a salary of hundreds of thousands of dollars to protest the network's exclusion of her friend and teacher. Anyway, Marilyn had had her fill of directors who didn't understand her. No amount of money could make her return to a Billy Wilder or a John Huston, much less a television technician of less stature.

A second disappointment was the Jean Harlow project. A movie biography was being planned about the platinum blonde to whom Marilyn had been compared so often. "I'm a natural for that one," she said securely. Jean Harlow was less the dumb blonde, more the brassy one. Nevertheless, Marilyn identified with this early movie sex symbol and deeply wanted the role. The Hollywood producers disagreed with her. Early on, they eliminated her from the running, she told me. After Marilyn died, the part eventually went to Carroll Baker, whose co-star was Marilyn's close friend Peter Lawford. The film was a failure.

At this point, Marilyn, worried about her age and beauty, began to panic over roles. She even considered, for a brief moment, throwing her hat in the ring for Billy Wilder's new movie *Irma la Douce*. She liked the part of the French prostitute with the heart of gold. All she wanted was a sincere apology from Billy Wilder and a promise of kindness in the future. Instead, the moment he learned that Marilyn was interested, the snide jokes started again. While Marilyn loved to laugh, she detested being ridiculed. It might have been the role of the century, but she just couldn't bring herself to work with Billy Wilder again.

The panic continued. Marilyn decided that she was hurting herself by remaining in New York. If the roles weren't coming to her, she would go where they were. She thus began spending more and more time in Hollywood, regardless of how much she disliked the place. In this case, business had to come first. She was desperate to get back into films, and even more desperate that her comeback role be a "sexy" one. Further-more, she wanted to finish off her contract with Twen-tieth Century-Fox, so she could start commanding the Elizabeth Taylor giant salaries she had convinced her-self she deserved now. As for Hollywood itself, all she looked forward to was Frank Sinatra. "At least, Frankie's there. It's his town. He won't let me be lonely."

One companion Frank did help her find was a new psychiatrist, a relative of his attorney. Marilyn was entranced by this man from the start. "Lena, Lena, I've finally found it. I've found a Jesus for myself," she told me breathlessly on her first trip back after meeting this doctor.

"A Jesus?"

"Yes, Lena. I call him Jesus. He's doing wonderful things for me."

"What?" I asked. Marilyn had gone to a lot of psychiatrists, but I never saw her so enthusiastic about any of them. Usually she returned from their sessions more depressed and confused than before she went. Now, she was breaking out the champagne to cele-brate this man's advice, not to try to forget it. "What does he do?"

"He listens to me."

"I do that."

"Oh, I know. You're my friend. But he's a doctor. And a genius. I'm going to take you out so you can see him. He'll help you."

"Don't be silly. I don't need a psychiatrist. I can't afford one."

"I'll pay," Marilyn said.

"You will not. I've got to worry about my family. I don't have time for a psychiatrist."

"You don't know what you're missing!"

"Maybe someday." I tried to get out of it as

gracefully as I could. "Tell me, what exactly does he do for you, besides listen?"

"He gives me courage. He makes me smart, makes me think. I can face anything with him. I'm not scared anymore. Now, nothing bothers me. I'm so happy."

Evidently, when Marilyn was in Hollywood, she saw this man every day. She sometimes called him several times a day from New York.

"What would you do if he took a vacation?" I asked her.

"I'd call him wherever he was."

"And what if you couldn't reach him?"

"I'd be in trouble."

This psychiatrist may have been good for Marilyn, but she grew completely dependent upon him. It was like an addiction. And she never talked of being well, so that she wouldn't need him again. That worried me. Although she seemed positive and outgoing, she had seemed the same way when things were smooth with Yves Montand. Should this doctor and Marilyn ever break, her comedown would be crushing.

What she learned through the psychiatrist, she told me, was that her marriage to Mr. Miller was the cause of many of her current problems. As a great intellect and playwright, he was too big a challenge for her. In trying to win his respect, she had become obsessed with the "serious dramatic actress" goal. This was false, it wasn't her. She would continue her acting lessons, and gradually improve her skills, but the movies she should concentrate on now were those that came most naturally to her—comedies, musicals, "fun" movies, nothing too serious. Above all, she said, she had to "be herself." "Whoever that is," she added with a giggle and a slightly puzzled look.

Because Marilyn was insecure about her thoughts as well as about her looks, I was very glad that she had someone who could reassure her in such a positive way that she was on the right track. Marilyn had never believed that she had good instincts. But now, this psychiatrist was telling her that her instincts were good—that she was right. He was building up her self-confidence in the process. For the first time, if she thought a role was right for her, she would speak up for it, rather than shyly holding back and letting others make her decisions for her. Marilyn said that this psychiatrist was by far the nicest, kindest doctor she had ever had. He really believed in her, she felt, and she believed in him.

When Marilyn called her psychiatrist "my Jesus," she wasn't being disrespectful. She simply had never followed any organized religion. She had shuttled around to so many foster homes, each with a different faith, that she had never had time to understand or adopt any particular one. She was understandably confused. "I didn't know much about religion," she said, "but I did learn how important it was to love one another. All religions say that." She liked Christian Science the most because her favorite guardian, Ana Lower, had been a Christian Scientist. It gave Marilyn a lot of inspiration for a while, but she eventually drifted away. "I was too weak," she admitted. "I *needed* these doctors and that medicine. I was so sick and I guess I just didn't have enough faith." When she married Mr. Miller she decided to become Jewish, mainly to please Mr. Miller's devout parents, whom she cared so much about. "Elizabeth Taylor converted, too. So we're both Jewish," she laughed. The only thing that bothered her about Judaism was its belief that there was no life after death. "Oh, I don't like that. I hope there's something else."

Yet somehow between the movies, the fights, and the depression, she never found time for any formal religion. Marilyn did believe in God, though, and frequently said little prayers, at odd times of the day. "I've got my own kind of religion," she said. "I pray for you all the time, Baby Lamb. I pray for Lee and Paula and Joe and Frankie, and Monty, and my mother . . . and even for my father, whoever he is."

Marilyn kept jetting back and forth between New York and Los Angeles, where she took an apartment. She told me that she saw Frank Sinatra all the time. While she disliked Hollywood immensely, she felt being out there was better for her movie career. Nevertheless, she still hadn't gotten a picture she liked. Perhaps the thing she liked least about Hollywood was that Joe DiMaggio didn't like it either. He was very reluctant to visit her there. He did see her in New York, though not as often as she would have liked.

On one trip from Hollywood, Marilyn returned with a bagful of brassieres. This was truly something new. The bras weren't ordinary ones. They were really just straps with the cups cut out. When I asked her why she bought them, she explained that she was worried about her breasts beginning to sag. She hoped these would hold them up, and since they were so skimpy, they were as close to wearing nothing as she could get. After about a week, she had thrown them all away. She just couldn't stand underwear, under any circumstances.

She had also purchased a large number of black and red lace panties. "Guys are supposed to like these," she smiled, holding them up to the light. "Who knows why?" These never got worn either. Instead, she threw them in a drawer, "for a special occasion." Marilyn had bought lots of new clothes during this period, too. Because she had lost weight, she fretted that she didn't look "sexy" enough. Consequently, she wore everything tighter and tighter.

I went out shopping with her many times. In the past, Marilyn preferred to have clothes sent up to try on, because she didn't like any attention. Now she loved it. In addition to the stores, she started coming out with me to walk Maf in the pretty park at the end of Fifty-seventh Street, overlooking the East River. While the old men and women who sat there gaped at her, and whispered, Marilyn just smiled. Everyone smiled back. She loved looking at the Queensboro Bridge, as its lights came on at dusk. It looked like a glittering necklace. There were tankers that sailed by so close you could almost touch them. To Marilyn, this was the most romantic spot in Manhattan. She wanted Joe DiMaggio to stroll with her here, but he always refused, just as he stuck to his back-door route via the service elevator. He *never* wanted any publicity.

Going shopping with Marilyn was an experience in itself. She would now get dressed up and made up almost as if she were going to a premiere. She didn't want to wear any disguise at all, but she compromised and wore her black wig. "Otherwise, they say there'll be a riot," she laughed. "Gee, that might be fun." Her favorite store was Bloomingdale's, not so much for the clothes as for all the crowds of men that ogled her. "I think they'd know me even if I were wearing a mask," she beamed. The old days when she would run for a back stairway were over. She'd talk to anyone.

I don't think she was all that serious about buying anything at Bloomingdale's. She'd just wander from one floor to another, seeing how big a mob she could attract. Whenever she really wanted to buy clothes, she would go to the ultrasedate Martha's on Park Avenue. Yet, even there, the snobbish clientele of society ladies seemed just as fascinated and eager to talk to Marilyn as the men on the street. She took this as a real compliment, though it was the men who mattered most.

In spite of all this attention, Marilyn was never fully self-confident about her appeal. Each day she'd spot a new line, a new wrinkle, and it would disturb her. I assured her she was as attractive as any woman, but that wasn't enough. She didn't believe her friends would tell her the truth. She had to test herself with strangers. To do this, she'd put on her black wig, a scarf and very little makeup, and go to sit at the bar at Manny Wolf's Chophouse on Third Avenue and Fiftieth Street. It was dark there. Marilyn must have had the most changeable looks of any woman on earth. She had so many hairdos and wore so much in the way of makeup, lipstick, false eyelashes, and the like, that you might not recognize her when she got up in the morning. Yet that unmade-up look was the real her. She was curious, and more than a little afraid, to see what men thought of her without all the movie star trappings. "I just want to seem like another woman. Not Marilyn. Then I'll see what people really think."

Marilyn was delighted with the results. She'd come home, usually before midnight and always alone. She didn't want to pick anyone up. She merely wanted to make sure that she could. Traveling salesmen, lawyers, businessmen, would all offer her drinks, and Marilyn relished describing the background and the approach of each one. Posing as a secretary, Marilyn was often "discovered." "They always half fall out of their chairs. One guy spilled a drink all over both of us. It was hilarious."

But on one crowded Friday night, no one even talked to Marilyn. She came home in tears. Then she drank her champagne and pored over every inch of her face in the mirror, crying all the while.

I insisted that she try again next week. "Anybody can have an off night," I said. She did try and the men flocked to her again. Her confidence was restored, though I realized what a tricky position she had placed herself in. One rejection could throw her into an awful depression. How I wished she had one man to be with her and comfort her—all the time. No woman ever needed a husband more. She realized this, too, and it made her even more desperate.

"Nobody's ever gonna marry me now, Lena. What good am I? I can't have kids. I can't cook. I've been divorced three times. Who would want me?"

"Millions of men," I answered.

"Yeah, but who would *love* me? Who?"

I knew that Joe DiMaggio loved her. Yet he was dead set against marriage. As for Frank Sinatra, he was linked with lots of women. Every time Marilyn heard about one she got very blue. Although she knew Frank was nearly impossible to catch, she hoped that she might overcome the odds. "Frankie's bound to want to settle down someday soon. Just wait." Unfortunately, until one of these men changed his mind, or until she met a new man who loved her as much, Marilyn would have to continue relying on brief periods of happiness with Joe and Frank, and upon the flattery of strangers and near strangers, to keep her spirits from caving in.

An encounter that did just that was my father's visit from Italy in late 1961. This was the man who wouldn't let me become a singer, because he said that singers, actresses, and prostitutes were all the same. My father was very straitlaced and old-fashioned in many ways, although underneath he had a wonderful sense of humor and knew how to have a good time. Regardless of his low opinion about entertainers, my father worshiped Marilyn Monroe. She was more to him than just an actress. He had written me begging for autographed pictures, records, anything. Now he was going to meet her in person. I think he was more excited by this than by seeing his children and grandchildren here in the States. My father wasn't the only strict type in my family who loved Marilyn. I had a cousin in Providence, Rhode Island, who was a priest. He kept an autographed copy of Marilyn's famous nude calendar right on his wall by his desk. "There's nothing dirty about a beautiful girl like that," he said.

From the way I had talked about my father, I think Marilyn assumed that he was a very crusty old man. She had promised to take him out to dinner, just the two of them. He spoke fairly good English, better than Yves Montand, so I wasn't worried about their communicating. Anyway, Marilyn could entertain anyone, whether the person spoke English or not. She was such a good listener that her companion, no matter what he spoke, would think she understood every word.

The big surprise, though, came more for Marilyn than my father. She had put on one of her looser, more sedate, beige cocktail dresses and had made a reservation at a formal French restaurant. But the moment she met my father, she decided to change everything. She saw he wasn't an old man at all. He was in his mid-fifties and was very handsome, tall, dark eyes, his once jet black hair streaked with gray. He looked very distinguished in his dark suit, very definitely her "type." After a few glasses of champagne, he loosened up completely, and had her laughing at all his jokes and his impressions of America. I could tell they were going to have great fun together.

Realizing that she looked much more conservative

than the mood she was in, Marilyn went back to her room and changed into the tight white pants and blouse she had tried to excite Monty Clift with. This time she tied the blouse into a sash, exposing her flat stomach. When she came back out, my father needed another big drink. This was the Marilyn he had been expecting.

Marilyn also changed her dinner plans. She asked me if she could take my father down to eat in Greenwich Village and later out dancing. She seemed worried about what my mother, home in Naples, would think.

"Don't be silly," I told her. "Go and enjoy yourselves. She wants him to have a good time in America."

Marilyn gave my father exactly that. When he didn't come home until three in the morning, I didn't worry. "I *love* America," my father nearly sang as he danced through the door. It took many cups of coffee to bring him back to earth. He couldn't believe that he had done the town with none other than Marilyn Monroe. I never asked my father *exactly* what happened. Whatever, for the rest of his life, he never stopped talking about how wonderful Marilyn was. "It's my luck he's married," Marilyn kidded me. "I'd love to be your mother."

But as soon as my father left, Marilyn got depressed again. It was the same when Joe left, or Frank left. She needed a man's company. That made her happy. Without it, all she had to fall back on was the telephone, and the airplane to Los Angeles and her psychiatrist. "Maybe I'll meet someone nice on the plane," she said, each time she left. I couldn't believe that Marilyn Monroe would have more trouble meeting the right man than most of my plain, average girlfriends. But she did. Being a great star was no guarantee of love at all.

Aside from Paula Strasberg and myself, Marilyn

had no other women she could confide in. Norman Rosten's wife, Hedda, was something of a friend, but when Mr. Miller left, it was a little awkward for Marilyn to see the Rostens without him. They were more his friends than hers. May Reis also left a few months after Mr. Miller did. May was very close to him, and I imagine it was difficult for her to continue working for one without the other. Her place was taken, for a while, by Marjorie Stengel, who had previously been secretary to Montgomery Clift.

Marjorie, who was about forty, was very sweet. She was tall and gangly, with dark bangs and a deep voice. She would dress in a gray skirt, white blouse, and low heels, almost like a uniform for a girls' school. It was a relief to have such a friendly girl working with us, since May Reis had been so cold and withdrawn. Marjorie's problem was that she was too friendly.

Marjorie's affectionate nature made Marilyn highly nervous. Marjorie would stand in the bedroom and stare wide-eyed at Marilyn's nakedness. She told Marilyn many times how beautiful her body was. Although Marjorie did her secretarial job quite well, it was clear that her real compensation was not money, but just being around Marilyn. Eventually, Marilyn got so uncomfortable that she decided that she and Marjorie should part company.

I still couldn't understand why Marjorie's presence disturbed her so until Marilyn confessed that she once had had an affair of her own with her first drama teacher, a foreign lady named Natasha Lytess, whom she lived with in her starlet days. Marilyn had looked up to her, and when she made her advances, Marilyn simply accepted them as part of her training. Also, Marilyn was pretty much all alone in those days. Any warmth shown to her, by any person, regardless of his or her sex, was welcomed and cherished. Marilyn needed to be loved—by anyone who was sincere.

"I was so confused back then, I'd let any guy, or girl, do what they wanted if I thought they were my friend. I let Natasha, but that was wrong. She wasn't like a guy. You know, just have a good time and that's that. She got really jealous about the men I saw, everything. She thought she was my husband. She was a great teacher, but that part of it ruined things for us. I got scared of her, had to get away." Marilyn said there was something about Marjorie that reminded her of Natasha: they were both skinny, ghostlike, and stared intensely. Marilyn couldn't afford to keep any bad memories around her. She had enough problems coping with the present.

Marjorie's place was taken over by young Pat Newcomb, from Marilyn's public relations agency. Pat seemed like an eager, efficient college girl and didn't threaten Marilyn at all. Pat was all business, seeing her role as mainly one of shielding Marilyn from the press, setting up interviews and photography sessions, making sure all her travel plans went smoothly. Sometimes she was too protective of Marilyn, who often got annoyed when she had a chance to meet the public and Pat steered her away from it. Frequently, Marilyn urged Pat to loosen up and have some champagne with her. "All work and no play . . ." she teased her. Pat wouldn't listen. She worked for an agency, not Marilyn herself, and took her job too seriously to have a good time.

Another woman who also came into Marilyn's life during this time was Mrs. Berneice Miracle. This was Marilyn's half-sister from Florida. Marilyn's mother had been married and divorced before she had Marilyn. Berneice was her daughter, though, like Marilyn,

Berneice wasn't raised by her mother. She had gone to live with her father's relatives in the South. Somehow, when Marilyn became famous, Berneice was able to get in touch with her. Marilyn, of course, was dying to meet this woman.

At first, Marilyn was skeptical. "Maybe she's making it all up, just to get money or something." May Reis, who was still there at the time, fueled Marilyn's doubts, particularly where the money was concerned. May's extreme caution made Marilyn mad at her. "It's easy for you to say, May." Marilyn made up her mind to see Berneice, and she wouldn't be swayed. "Hell, it's my money. What good is it doing me? I have a right to have a family. Everyone else does." The moment she met Berneice, Marilyn was convinced this was her real relative. "Her blood's the same as mine. Imagine!" Marilyn announced joyfully. Smothering Berneice with kisses, Marilyn held her and wouldn't let her go. "My sister!" Berneice, in her forties, was also a blonde, even blonder naturally than Marilyn. She was slightly shorter and thinner, yet her figure was definitely on the voluptuous side. Even their faces bore a resemblance. When they sat in the apartment, Marilyn kept looking at her in amazement. "Gee, you're really my sister. My sister," Marilyn repeated.

Although Marilyn and Berneice didn't have very much in common, Marilyn was desperate to get to know her. She invited Berneice and her husband for a lavish ten-day trip to New York, put them up at an expensive hotel, hired a chauffeur to drive them around to see the sights (with Marilyn as the proud tour guide), and took them to famous restaurants every day for both lunch and dinner. She even sent Berneice to her favorite stores for clothes and to Kenneth for the complete beauty treatment. Marilyn admitted secretly that she wanted her half sister "to look just like me."

Despite the royal treatment, Berneice wasn't the glamour-queen type. She and her husband were anything but rich. They were plain people. Mr. Miracle, I believe, was either a farmer or a laborer. Marilyn insisted on giving them a large sum of money, "so they can live better and educate their kids." In a way, Berneice seemed far shyer than Marilyn, who was now in an outgoing phase. All the hustle and glitter of Manhattan seemed to scare Berneice. She seemed in a daze, caused by New York as well as by Marilyn. It wasn't easy for her to come to grips with having a famous movie star for a long-lost sister.

The two women—one a world celebrity, the other a housewife—didn't have much to say to each other, except to compare childhoods. "At least you lived with relatives," Marilyn told Berneice, when she complained about her problems growing up. Yet the way Marilyn sat at attention holding Berneice's hand and listening to every detail about where Berneice shopped in Florida, what she cooked, how she ran her home and raised her sons, made me think that Marilyn could easily be tempted to trade in all her fame and become a housewife, too. Otherwise, Berneice knew little about movies and movies were almost all that Marilyn knew about.

Neither of the women could talk about their mother, as Berneice seemed to know even less about her than Marilyn did. Marilyn's own feelings about her mother were mixed. When I asked her why she didn't bring her to New York to be with her, she answered, " 'Cause she's cuckoo." Marilyn felt her mother was better off in the California sanitarium, where, Marilyn said, she was constantly sending money for her mother's care. There was still a trace of bitterness over her mother's abandoning her to foster homes as a child. "She didn't want to see me then. Why should she now?" Then in the next breath, Marilyn, eyes moist, would say, "I wish she could get well, so we could talk. It would be great to have a real mother, right here. And if Berneice lived in New York, too, we all could live like a regular family. . . . We could have dinner on Sunday, go for drives, to plays. . . . Aw, it's fun to dream, isn't it?"

Marilyn kept on dreaming. She wanted to be cared for by everyone and especially by someone in particular. She dreamt of being happy, of being in love. At the same time, she wouldn't forget her career. Now she was a completely independent woman. She didn't have to live to please Mr. Miller or to measure up to what she thought he expected of her. She could follow her own instincts, do what she believed was right. As Marilyn entered the last year of her life, she was feeling stronger and more optimistic than ever. On her thirty-fifth birthday, she told me, "Baby Lamb, this year things are going to be better. Things are going to work out. I can feel it. This is gonna be my year."

10

At first, it seemed that Marilyn was right that the year ahead was going to be hers. A couple of months after her birthday in June, she told me that she thought Frank Sinatra was going to marry her. He hadn't asked her, but Marilyn's intuition was usually right. "He's almost ready," she announced in triumph.

"But what about Joe?" I asked.

"He'll never marry me again. Never. He loves me, but that's it. We can't agree about the movies." Frank, on the other hand, was in the same business as she was. "Frankie wouldn't expect me to be a housewife. We can both have our careers. It'll be perfect . . . I hope." She crossed the fingers of both her hands and held them in the air. Then she closed her eyes, making a wish to herself. "Let me be lucky . . . just once."

Because of Frank, Marilyn wanted to be in Hollywood as much as possible. I had always talked about going to visit there. I wanted to see where the movies

were made and where the stars lived. From what I had
read, it seemed like a kind of paradise to me. Marilyn
thought that idea was hilarious. "Paradise?" she
roared. "Hollywood is shit. It's horrible. I'll take you
out there, Lena. If you really want to go, I'll show it to
you. Maybe you will like it. Who knows? I sure
don't."

Marilyn told me that Los Angeles, at least Beverly
Hills, Bel Air, and other suburbs where the show
business people lived, was beautiful. There were
mountains, ocean, palm trees, perfect weather. But
most of the place, she explained, was full of hamburger
stands, used-car lots, and ugly, low buildings that all
looked like motels. The architecture, though, wasn't
what troubled Marilyn. It was her terrible memories of
growing up there. "Los Angeles is a nightmare when
you're poor. You see the movie stars and what they
have, then you look at what you have. It makes you
sick." Marilyn also would never forget being mis-
treated and misunderstood by the powerful studio
executives who lived in those fantastic houses. To her,
they were Los Angeles.

When I suggested that she could have her own
house and pool, bigger and better than those of any of
the men who had hurt her, she shook her head. "Who
wants it? I don't want to live near them. I don't want to
see them. I love New York. This is my home now. It's
gonna stay my home. I hope I can get Frankie to come
back here, but he doesn't feel like I do about L.A. He
was always a winner there. He wasn't kicked around
the way I was." Still, Marilyn said that if she married
Frank, she could take Los Angeles, memories and all.
She'd still keep the New York apartment as an escape
valve. As she put it, "Frankie and I can be happy
anywhere."

One morning in September, 1961, I got an excited call from California. "You're coming out, Baby Lamb. Your dream's come true. I'm gonna show you Hollywood." Marilyn was going to have me fly out to bring her a special dress, which she wanted to wear to a big Hollywood ball she was going to with Frank. "Everybody's gonna be there," Marilyn said. Not only did she want to look good for the film world, she wanted to look good for Frank. "He likes me best when I'm all dressed up." She said she had bought some dresses in Beverly Hills, but had decided they weren't "glamorous enough for Frankie." She was so close to a proposal, she felt, that she didn't want to take any risks.

The dress which I was to bring was a sequined emerald green evening gown, which Marilyn had just had made for herself. It costs $3000. She didn't think it was going to be ready in time for this affair. When she learned that it was finished, she insisted on having it. "I've already told Frankie and he's all excited about seeing me in it. But the best thing of all, Lena, is that you can come out. I can't wait to see you."

I rushed home and packed, then returned to the apartment to get Marilyn's dress all ready. When Pat Newcomb handed me my first-class ticket on the flight to Los Angeles, she told me that I was going to have a special escort on the plane to make sure I didn't get lost. She wouldn't tell me who it was, other than I would have a big surprise.

My husband took me to the airport. I wished that he could be with me, but he had to work. He couldn't change his vacation plans on such short notice. When the cabin attendant escorted me to my seat, there was a man sitting beside me looking out the window. He turned around. It was Henry Fonda. Pat's publicity firm was so powerful that it must have been able to arrange *anything,* including putting me next to a movie star. What a way to go to Hollywood!

I couldn't have dreamed of a nicer traveling companion. Between his stories about the movies, the champagne, the caviar, and the other treats of flying first class, the trip was over far too soon. It was almost six in the morning, New York time, and I wasn't even tired. Here I was in Los Angeles. As we landed, Mr. Fonda warned me that I might be disappointed with the place. He said the trip to Hollywood would make me glad I lived in New York. I couldn't understand why so many of the stars Marilyn knew disliked Hollywood as much as she did. They all seemed to prefer New York. More fun, more to do, more exciting people—these were the reasons they gave. But now, I was here, and the soft, balmy night air felt wonderful to me.

Marilyn's chauffeur was waiting for me at the airport. After thanking and saying good-bye to Mr. Fonda, I was driven to the Beverly Wilshire Hotel, where Marilyn had reserved me an elegant suite, all in blue, my favorite color. I would have loved to stay with Marilyn, but she insisted on the hotel. It was one of the most luxurious in the country, and she stressed how much I'd enjoy the beautiful furniture, the room service, the fancy shops, the celebrities in the lobby. "It'll be a real vacation for you, Lena."

Marilyn had complained that her apartment was just a place for her to sleep. It was too small and uncomfortable to entertain houseguests, though I wouldn't have minded sleeping on the couch at all. However, Marilyn already had one special guest to worry about. Because Marilyn was so thrilled that she and Frank Sinatra were growing closer every day, I was sure that she didn't need anyone else around to disrupt the romantic atmosphere she was trying to create.

The hotel was every bit as lovely as Marilyn had described. Despite my queen-size bed and soft linens, I couldn't seem to fall asleep. It felt strange being in this huge room all by myself. If only my husband were here to share this with me. I lay awake until the brilliant California sun flooded the room, thinking of my family and thinking of Marilyn. I couldn't wait to see her. I was too excited to sleep. The next morning, after breakfast in bed, the chauffeur drove me to Marilyn's. The bright sunshine and lush greenery amazed me. I was so used to grim, gray New York that I thought that's how everyone lived. I was wrong.

Yet in contrast to Beverly Hills's palatial homes and brilliant colors, Marilyn's place was just as gloomy as her New York apartment. The drapes were closed. The main piece of furniture was Marilyn's giant bed. The few chairs and lamps confirmed Marilyn's insistence that this was only a temporary residence.

But the house wasn't what mattered. There was Marilyn, throwing her arms around me. "Baby Lamb, you made it! You're here! Was the trip O.K.?" She had on her favorite white terry-cloth robe and was drinking champagne. We might as well have been in New York. She was delighted that I had sat with Henry Fonda and promised that she'd give Pat Newcomb a "big tip" for arranging it. "She's really on the ball," Marilyn said.

As soon as Marilyn saw I was well taken care of, she ripped open the package containing her dress. She took off her robe, and put the gown on. She looked spectacular. "Boy, wait till Frankie sees this!" she boasted, looking at herself in the mirror for at least a half hour. "Lena, make me some stuffed peppers, please," she begged me, although it was still morning.

There wasn't enough food in the kitchen to make anything, and I began writing a shopping list to go out. Then Marilyn changed her mind. She decided not to eat all that day. "I want to look skinny for Frankie."

So, instead of food, Marilyn just drank champagne, as usual. Meanwhile, she let her West Coast hairdresser and makeup people prepare her for the big evening. Marilyn announced that I would be going with her. I was shocked. "I can't go," I blurted.

"Yes, you can. You will," she insisted. She had the chauffeur take me back to the Beverly Wilshire to dress. She said I didn't need an evening gown. She *had* to dress but not everybody else did. By the time I returned, Marilyn was almost ready. She was always on time, or even early, where Frank was concerned.

Finally, Frank arrived, in full evening dress. While he didn't have much hair and was getting slightly paunchy, he seemed far more dashing than he ever had in pictures. I opened the door for him, but before we could even introduce ourselves, Marilyn flew into the room like an exotic tropical bird, her platinum hair and green-sequined dress electrifying the drab apartment. Frank's face lit up, too. He was clearly thrilled by the way she looked. With a breathless "Frankie!" she embraced him. They kissed like two people truly in love. They slowly drew apart to admire each other, Marilyn stroking the satin lapel of Frank's dinner jacket.

Then Frank told Marilyn to close her eyes. He pulled a box out of his pocket and clipped two gorgeous emerald earrings on Marilyn's ears. He planted a kiss on each ear in the process. Frank told her to open her eyes, and led her to a mirror, his arm around her waist. "Oh, Frankie! Frankie!" Marilyn was speechless. They kissed again, so passionately this time that I was embarrassed to be standing by. Marilyn began gushing about how beautiful the earrings were. Frank just laughed, and told her they ought to be. They cost $35,000, he said. I was surprised that he mentioned what they cost, but Marilyn later told me, "Frankie and I don't keep any secrets from each other." When Marilyn heard the price, she nearly fainted. The kissing began again.

Suddenly, Marilyn noticed me in the mirror. "Baby Lamb!" she exclaimed. "Look! Look at these! Come here. Lena Pepitone, meet Frank Sinatra." I came over and shook Frank's hand. He drew me closer and hugged me. He asked me what I thought about the earrings. "Beautiful," was all I could say. Frank told me how much he had heard about me, that Marilyn never stopped talking about me, and that I should move out to California to be with her. *That*, he thought, would make her like Los Angeles better.

"Don't listen to Frankie. We're gonna stay in New York. He can come there," Marilyn laughed.

Frank kept insisting. How could I put up with the weather, the noise, and the dirt? He'd get my husband a good job, and we'd move out. California was great, he said. Besides, he'd heard too many good things about my cooking. Having to go back to New York every time he wanted great Italian meals was getting to be too much trouble for him. Marilyn needed me, and he needed me, too. I was really flattered.

Two limousines took us to the benefit on Sunset Boulevard, one for Marilyn and Frank, the other for myself and Lydia, a young girl who worked for Marilyn and whom Marilyn wanted to keep me company. "I would have fixed you up with a handsome actor for a date, but I didn't want your Joe to get jealous. It's bad enough leaving him alone," Marilyn said. "There'll be so many photographers, they might have taken your picture with the guy and Joe would never

have forgiven me." I told her not to apologize; there
was sure to be enough excitement to keep me oc-
cupied.

And there was. Nearly every star in Hollywood
seemed to be there. Yet Marilyn and Frank seemed to
be the center of attention. Every man wanted to kiss
her; every woman wanted to kiss him. Even Billy
Wilder and Tony Curtis seemed to have been forgiven
that evening. Marilyn greeted them as if they were the
greatest of friends. The only person she didn't talk to
was Elizabeth Taylor. I didn't see her, but Marilyn
knew she would be there. That was one more reason
for sending for her emerald dress. She wanted to be the
most beautiful star in the house. She was.

Despite all the attention she was getting, Marilyn
didn't forget me. After the ceremonies were over and
the dancing began, she came to the table where Lydia
and I were sitting and took us around to get everyone's
autograph. At the end of the evening, Marilyn and
Frank saw me off to my hotel before going home
together. She was as happy as I had ever seen her.
"See you tomorrow, Lena . . . in the afternoon. I'm
going to sleep real late." As she kissed me good night,
she pinched me and gave me a wicked wink. She
wanted me to know how much fun she was having.

The next few days, the chauffeur gave me the grand
tour of Los Angeles—the stars' homes, the movie
studios, Grauman's Chinese Theatre with the stars'
footprints, the Pacific beaches, the Hollywood Bowl,
the fancy stores of Beverly Hills. The only thing I
missed was Disneyland. This was on purpose. I would
have been sad going there alone, knowing how much
my little Joey and Johnny would have enjoyed it.
Marilyn promised that she'd have my whole family for
a visit next summer when the kids were out of school.
"I'll go with you then. I've never been to Disneyland,

either," she said. I knew how much she loved my boys and the kick she'd get in taking them on all the rides.

When I wasn't sight-seeing, I was at Marilyn's, cooking and talking. Each day I was there she had the beauty people in, for she was seeing Frank every night. "Any day now," she whispered to me, referring to the proposal she'd been praying for. "Everything's working out just right. The dress was perfect. Frankie loved it!" Marilyn couldn't thank me enough for bringing it out. I was a little disappointed that Marilyn couldn't come along with me and the chauffeur, but she was too exhausted, she said, from the nights before. She wanted to be in top form for Frank, and she knew I understood this.

Aside from her evenings with Frank, Marilyn's life in California seemed identical to her life in New York. She didn't read, didn't watch television, didn't go anywhere. Although the sun was always shining, Marilyn was as pale as ever. She didn't like to go outside during the day. She never exercised. No wonder the California outdoor life had no appeal for her. Sleeping, champagne, Sinatra records, telephone calls, visits to her psychiatrist, playing with her dog Maf, trying on clothes—these took up almost all of Marilyn's time. While I was there, I didn't see Marilyn take a single pill. With Frank, she didn't need any. But when I was straightening up, in her bathroom, I found a medicine cabinet overflowing with prescriptions, as well as a drawerful by her bed. In New York, she depended upon these drugs to relax and to sleep. I hoped that she'd never have to take them again.

Marilyn and I had a glass of champagne together before I left. I couldn't stop thanking her for the wonderful trip I had had. She couldn't stop thanking me for coming. "You're my good luck charm, Lena," she said, sticking an envelope into my pocketbook as we hugged good-bye. "Don't open it until you're on the plane, and give Joe and the boys a big kiss for me." She said she'd be back in New York as soon as things with Frank and the movies were worked out. When I opened the envelope, I found five hundred-dollar bills. Money was her way of saying thank you and that she cared. I knew she meant it.

Marilyn returned to New York more quickly than I would have guessed. Sadly, nothing had worked out. Frank had not proposed, and she still hadn't found the right film for herself. She got depressed and very nervous. Again, she started eating all the time and taking pills to sleep. Things got even worse when Marilyn found out that Frank was going out with Juliet Prowse, a stunning dancer from South Africa who was only in her twenties. This made Marilyn feel old—far older than she looked.

Although Juliet Prowse was just breaking in as an actress, she was already becoming famous for her legs. They were supposed to be the most beautiful in Hollywood, Marilyn told me. Now Marilyn, who had never paid much attention to her legs, couldn't stop looking at them. "They're too short and fat," she moaned, with a look of disgust. "They're horrible." She was constantly on the phone, asking everyone she knew "how bad" her legs were. Of course, they weren't, but that didn't matter. Legs and age were the only things Juliet Prowse could ever possibly have on her. "How could Frankie do this?" Marilyn despaired. Not that Frank had disappeared from Marilyn's life. He still called her, he still saw her. They both cared the world for each other. The only difference was that Marilyn had realized that they would never marry. It hurt deeply, but Frank was one friend Marilyn would never give up. "I can't tie him down, not Frankie, but I'll always love him."

Frank's apparent preference for a younger woman did, however, drive Marilyn into a terrible bout of insecurity. With Frank, she was Queen of Hollywood. Without him, she saw herself as a has-been. While Marilyn rarely ever lashed out against any woman star other than Elizabeth Taylor, she now began criticizing all the young, blonde "imitation Marilyns" that Hollywood was grooming, she feared, to replace her. She was particularly harsh about Jayne Mansfield, who, she believed, had had an operation to enlarge her breasts. "At least I'm real," Marilyn said. But getting older clearly terrified her. She told me that she had nightmares about being a little old lady, all alone in an asylum, locked in a cell. She felt she would be cursed for "abandoning" her mother. "I started with nothing. I'm going to end up with nothing," she wept.

The only thing Marilyn had to look forward to in New York were the acting classes with Lee Strasberg. She was dedicated to him and to learning the craft others had made fun of her for. Yet she was rapidly losing confidence that she could ever become a great actress. Even if she did, she felt that Hollywood would never give her a chance. The big parts were not being offered to her.

She was still in shock about Frank and always sad that things could never work out with Joe DiMaggio, who continued to see her and support her. She needed more from him—a total commitment, which he wouldn't give. Every day in New York, then, grew more and more disheartening. If only for a change of bedrooms and to see her psychiatrist, Marilyn flew back to California.

Then, miraculously, things improved. Marilyn met a Mexican movie producer named José Bolanos. I'm not sure exactly how or where they met; I do know that Marilyn fell madly in love with him. No one could have been more ready to fall in love than Marilyn was. Bolanos was Marilyn's age—thirty-five—and as she described him, was dark, intense, powerful, and in the one word she used most often, a "man." He wasn't at all handsome, she said. "None of my men are." When I asked her why he was so special, she answered, "His unbelievable manners. And he's the greatest lover in the whole wide world!"

Bolanos had been a bullfighter, a dashing matador, who was "discovered" by an aging Mexican movie star who got him into films. "I hear he makes some of the worst movies in Mexico," Marilyn laughed. "Silly romances. But what do I care? Everything else he does is incredible."

The "everything else" referred to Bolanos's total attention to Marilyn and his passion for her. When she thought she was going to marry Frank, Marilyn had once compared Frank's amorous abilities to those of Joe DiMaggio. "Joe just sweeps you off your feet without even trying. But Frankie, he doesn't sweep you, he knocks you over. He goes wild. God, does that guy *love* women." According to Marilyn, no man ever got more excited over her than Frank. And with all her anxieties over aging and losing her sex appeal, Frank's attention was exactly what she needed to assure her she was as desirable as ever. José Bolanos picked up where Frank left off, making her feel even more desirable. "Like I'm the only woman on earth," she glowed.

Bolanos also scared her. "One minute he's laughing, then he starts thinking about something and goes into a crazy mood. I never know what he's thinking. And if he sees another man even looking at me, he wants to kill him. If I looked back, gee, I don't know what he'd do to me. But it's exciting, being scared. It's sexy. I love it." Now everything in Marilyn's life had to be Mexican. She bought Latin records and a book about how to do dances like the rhumba and the samba. She talked about a Spanish course. She even purchased a little Mexican-type house to live in which she described as her "Los Angeles love nest" for her and José. After buying the house, she took a special shopping trip to Mexico, supposedly to furnish the house. Yet, I knew how little Marilyn cared about interior decorating. The trip was nothing other than an excuse to be with José Bolanos. "All we did was dance, drink, and make love," Marilyn giggled when she returned to New York.

This year for Marilyn was either all up or all down. Now was up. In addition to her romance with José, she had finally found a comedy, *Something's Got to Give*. She was to play a wife whose husband had given her up for dead. She wasn't. After several years, she returns, finding her husband about to get married again. The original version, *My Favorite Wife*, made twenty years before with Cary Grant, was a smash. Marilyn loved the story and felt she could repeat the success. Her husband was to be played by Dean Martin, one of Frank Sinatra's best friends, and a star Marilyn was crazy about. The movie, in a way, would be like a family affair.

Furthermore, with this picture, Marilyn would be close to fulfilling her contract duties toward Twentieth Century-Fox. Then she could make movies entirely on her own, at an Elizabeth Taylor salary or higher. Marilyn told me that negotiations were under way for her to receive a new contract from another production company for eleven million dollars. She would go to Italy, Austria, and other European countries to make films. Foreign locations had always been one of her fantasies. We had talked about going to Italy together for years. Now it looked very real and she begged me to travel with her, at least some of the time. I discussed it with my husband and relatives, who said they'd be delighted to take care of the boys while I was gone. This would be the chance of a lifetime. They were generous enough not to want me to miss it. Besides, they had all met Marilyn and treated her like a family member. "*She* needs you most of all," they said. "You've *got* to help her."

Something's Got to Give looked as if it were going to be an easy, fun production. However, when the shooting began in April, Marilyn's down phase started again. Marilyn and José Bolanos had been partying so hard that her resistance was very low. Always prone to colds, Marilyn picked up some Mexican virus, which she just couldn't seem to get rid of. The lateness, missed lines, missed days that the entire industry had come to associate with Marilyn began all over. "I can't help it," she told me over the phone. "It's just my luck. Whenever I make a movie, I get sick."

Marilyn continued complaining about the virus and the high fever, which kept her off the film set for so much time. She was less worried about herself, though, than about what the others in the film were thinking and saying. There were all sorts of rumors that Marilyn's delays were bankrupting Twentieth Century-Fox. "Shit!" Marilyn said. "It's not fair. Why don't they ever blame her?" "Her" was Elizabeth Taylor. The movie *Cleopatra,* for which Taylor was being paid a million dollars, was millions more over its budget. Elizabeth Taylor had been sick, too, delaying her production far, far longer than Marilyn ever had delayed hers. Marilyn was outraged that no one accused Elizabeth Taylor of making up illnesses. "If she can be sick, why can't I?" As Marilyn saw it, Elizabeth Taylor was Twentieth Century-Fox's favorite pet; Marilyn was their slave.

Sick or not, Marilyn came back to New York in the middle of May to sing "Happy Birthday" to President John F. Kennedy at a huge celebration the Democratic party was having at Madison Square Garden. The Kennedy family was another subject of rumors, which Marilyn denied. It was, and has been, frequently whispered that Marilyn was having an affair with President Kennedy, or his brother Bobby, or both. Marilyn didn't get mad at these rumors, though. She just laughed. The Kennedys, whom she had met through Frank Sinatra's friend Peter Lawford (then the husband of a Kennedy sister, Pat), were "cute," Marilyn said. She liked them because they were funny and smart. "But they're not my type. They're boys." Marilyn was still very much in love with her "man," José Bolanos. He seemed as different from the Kennedys as one could be.

Marilyn knew very little about politics, and cared less. For example, all the excitement about Cuba and Communism didn't affect her at all. To Marilyn, Castro was a convertible sofa, not a dictator. Because she didn't read the paper or listen to the radio, she didn't know the Bay of Pigs invasion ever occurred. I remember telling her what a wonderful President John Kennedy was. All she could say was, "Well, he doesn't *look* like a President. He's too young." She seemed to think that every President was supposed to look like Abraham Lincoln.

She got to know the Kennedys far better at parties that Peter Lawford gave. Frank Sinatra and his friends like Lawford, Dean Martin, and Sammy Davis, Jr., were known around Hollywood as the "Rat Pack." They had been very active in helping John Kennedy get elected and he, in turn, was a close friend of theirs. The Kennedys seemed to enjoy the movie world and their base in Hollywood was the house of their brother-in-law, Peter Lawford. Lawford's was also one of the few places Marilyn ever went out to.

Marilyn spoke much more about John Kennedy than about Bobby. If he didn't look like her idea of a President, he didn't act like one either. At least around Marilyn. He was always telling her dirty jokes, pinching her, and squeezing her, she said. "That big tease," she laughed affectionately. She told me that President Kennedy was always putting his hand on her thigh. One night, under the dinner table, he kept going. But when he discovered she wasn't wearing any panties, he pulled back and turned red. "He hadn't counted on going that far," Marilyn grinned.

Marilyn could never quite figure out why the fun-loving President would be married to the woman Marilyn called "the statue." "I bet he doesn't put his hand up her dress," she smiled. "I bet no one does. Is she ever stiff!" Marilyn thought that President Kennedy probably married Jacqueline "because their families made them." That was how rich, Eastern, Ivy League types got married, Marilyn assumed. "I feel sorry for them. Locked into a marriage I bet neither of them likes. I can tell he's not in love. Not with her. Well, maybe she likes it. Maybe it's nice being the First Lady. I'll never know."

Marilyn may have had fun with the Kennedys, but as far as a romance was concerned, she never mentioned it. Getting to sing for the President, for the whole country to see, was a giant honor for Marilyn. *She* was asked, not Elizabeth Taylor. "That's because you're the biggest star of all," I told her, when she arrived back on Fifty-seventh Street. For once, she didn't disagree. If Marilyn was worried about the public forgetting her, she needn't have worried any more.

In leaving the movie set for this event, Marilyn had

another, more important motive that was far less selfish than all the publicity she would earn. She wanted to introduce Arthur Miller's father to her friend, the President of the United States. Even after the divorce, the elder Mr. Miller had stayed on Marilyn's side. He loved Marilyn and had told her to "always think of me as your father." That touched her deeply, making her cry whenever she mentioned what he said. Mr. Miller's wife had died and Marilyn wanted to do everything she could to cheer him up. "He's a wonderful man. Meeting the President will be the biggest thrill for him. He means more to me than any picture."

In her skintight, beaded evening dress, Marilyn may have looked like an odd companion for the quiet, gentle Mr. Miller, a head shorter than his son Arthur, whom Marilyn never mentioned anymore. The cute little man was beaming ear to ear. The evening went perfectly. The next day the whole country was talking about Marilyn's tribute to the President. No one had ever sung "Happy Birthday" like that. Everyone was delighted, that is, except Twentieth Century-Fox. When Marilyn returned to California, she could feel the mounting ill will toward her on the set. "They all hate me," she said over the phone, referring to the film executives who were producing the film. There was talk about replacing Marilyn with another actress. That made her furious. "They think I'm awful—for doing nothing. I'd like to really give them *something* to get mad about." It wasn't like Marilyn to antagonize people deliberately, for she wanted so much for everyone to like her. This time, though, she had heard too much gossip.

Now Marilyn did give the studio something to talk about. This was the famous scene in the swimming pool. In spite of her lingering virus, Marilyn was determined to prove that she wasn't afraid to work, even if it meant going swimming with a fever. I warned her to get well first; she wouldn't listen. In the scene, Marilyn was supposed to be wearing a flesh-colored swimming suit. "I decided then and there that the whole movie was as phony as that 'naked suit.' So I said the hell with it, and took it off. You shoulda seen everyone."

I knew that Marilyn had been very pleased with her figure when she was last in New York. For the first time in months, she could look in the mirror and smile, instead of lamenting about the signs of age. She was youthful, slender, and had absolutely nothing to hide. Marilyn didn't care, either, that photographers were snapping away for the world to see. Delighted with her body for once, she was thrilled about the whole experience. After seeing the photos, she was even happier. "I never realized how good I looked. I mean, years and years younger. Wow! That pool was the best thing about the damn movie—by far," she said.

Marilyn's nudity was the last straw for Twentieth Century-Fox. A few days later in June, Marilyn was fired. She had just celebrated her thirty-sixth birthday, June 1, with a party on the set. "They gave it, but they sure didn't mean it," Marilyn said afterward. "They wanted me out. I could tell." The idea of anybody, even Twentieth Century-Fox, "firing" Marilyn Monroe was a little ridiculous. If they didn't want her, every other studio did. Marilyn had been feeling very sure of herself recently—the Kennedy gala, the pool photos, the eleven-million-dollar-contract offer, José Bolanos. Being fired by the studio she detested didn't bother her at all. "Good riddance!" she declared.

The main thing she was unhappy about was being unable to continue working with her co-stars Dean Martin and Wally Cox, both of whom she liked a great deal. When the studio announced that Marilyn would be replaced by Lee Remick, Dean Martin quit in protest. He had signed on only because of Marilyn; he would only work if Marilyn were back. His actions made Marilyn feel very good. "He's a friend, a real friend," Marilyn told me.

Marilyn thought it was funny that when the studio sued Dean for millions, he sued them right back and for twice as much. "That'll show them." The studio also talked of suing Marilyn. "I'll sue them right back, too," she snapped, "for God knows how much." Marilyn was hurt to hear that all the details of her supposed unreliability were being dragged out in newspapers and magazines around the country. She didn't want her fans to resent her. "They're trying to make everyone hate me," she said. "If they can't make money by using me, they want to wreck my career so no one can. Animals!"

Despite all the name-calling, Marilyn was not depressed. She was angry. She believed enough in herself to fight back. Perhaps her psychiatrist had really done her good. She definitely wasn't scared anymore. Within a month, she won. Twentieth Century-Fox changed its decision. Marilyn won an apology. The movie would continue. Even though she wouldn't have cared if she never saw the script again, Dean Martin wanted her and she was loyal to him. During the showdown, Dean had left town for a nightclub tour. He was due to return in September. The shooting would resume then.

The rest of the summer belonged to Marilyn. She flew back to New York for more classes with Lee Strasberg and was feeling quite good about her work with him. After one particular rehearsal, her fellow students at the Actors' Studio had loudly applauded her. "When they clapped for me, I could tell they meant it," Marilyn said. No one was quicker to sense false praise than she was. She knew she had done a fine job. She was besieged with proposals for plays, for Las Vegas shows, for nightclubs, for movies. There was too much. She couldn't make up her mind. And, anyhow, her mind was less on her career than on José Bolanos.

Marilyn didn't stay in New York for long. She flew back to Los Angeles to be close to José, who, she said, flew up very often to be with her. She didn't want anyone to know very much, if anything, about their affair. Publicity, she felt, had ruined things with both Joe DiMaggio and Arthur Miller. "José doesn't want to be part of a sideshow. He'd leave if he was. I know him." She said that in California they rarely went out and never to places where she'd be recognized. They would go to her house, his hotel, or a drive-in restaurant or movie in some distant part of L.A., or to a beach at night. Anywhere to be alone, out of the public eye.

The privacy seemed to be effective. Near the end of July, Marilyn flew home to New York for a couple of days with exciting news. "He asked me to marry him. I can't believe it." I kissed her and congratulated her with all my heart. "I don't know what to say." Her big smile vanished, as she thought for a long while. "I mean . . . well, we haven't really talked about it, what José thinks of my career, where he wants to live. Lena, he's even more jealous than Joe. He might want me to get out of movies, too. Wouldn't that be something? And what if I had to live in Mexico? What am I going to do? I love him."

Marilyn's trip to New York was taken up with some business meetings, clothes purchases, and sleeping. "There's no other bed like this one. I just can't sleep the same out there. I'll be so happy to get back here for good." When I asked her about her new house, she said, "That's nothing. Just someplace of my own when I'm making movies. I'm sick of hotels. You'll see it. It's your house, too." Marilyn apologized over and over for not having my family out for Disneyland, as we had planned. She hadn't counted on the crisis with the studio. "That messed up everything. Next summer, I promise, Baby Lamb."

I stayed with Marilyn late each night, making her different kinds of pasta and veal dishes. "You could starve to death out there," she said, wishing that I could be with her in California. She had a housekeeper, an older woman whom her psychiatrist had recommended, but Marilyn didn't feel at ease with her. "She's like a spy for him. Watches me all the time; I bet she reports on me. She's creepy," Marilyn said. "I could never be friends with her. Oh, it's so lonely out there. If it wasn't for José and the telephone . . ."

Marilyn didn't take a pill during her entire visit, though she did drink more champagne than usual. She was nervous, very nervous, about what to do about José Bolanos. As she was going through her closets, she saw the picture of Joe DiMaggio, and suddenly began weeping. "If it could have only worked out. . . . Why, why didn't it? It's insane . . . two people who love each other and won't get married. Maybe if I wait, Joe'll . . . but if he doesn't, then José might leave . . . and there I am again, with zero. And getting older every day." The champagne kept flowing. "Oh, this is so mixed up. I don't know."

I suggested that maybe if Marilyn told Joe about José, Joe might finally give in. "Never!" Marilyn shouted. "He'd just get mad. I know what he'd say. He'd call José a gigolo or something awful. Joe doesn't think any man can love me except him. He's my best friend in the world. I don't want to lose him. I don't want to lose José. I don't want to lose anyone. Oh, help me, somebody," she cried, hugging her pillows to her chest.

"What about the psychiatrists?" I asked. "I thought they could help."

"No. They're just getting me more confused. Sometimes I think they're full of shit. You were right, Lena. I don't need a psychiatrist, I need a man. The right man. I think I've got him, but how can I be sure?"

"Give it time," I urged her. "He's not rushing you, is he?"

"Not really. But he's so moody, he could change his mind tomorrow. I never know what's with him. You're right. We can wait. If he loves me, he'll wait. . . . Won't he?"

"Sure," I said.

Marilyn may have been mixed up, but she certainly wasn't unhappy. When she left in her white cotton pants and blouse, she looked like a beautiful girl in her mid-twenties. Her hair was bouncy, her nails glowed, she even had the beginnings of a California tan from sitting around her pool. She had told me that her nude pictures were going to be in *Playboy*. Other pictures were going to appear in *Vogue*, still more in *Life*. She had all the magazines covered. She loved it. "I'll never be fat again," she laughed. "It doesn't pay." Marilyn gave me a long embrace while we waited for the elevator. "Take care of everything, Lena. I'll probably be back sooner than you think . . . with lots of good news, I hope. Wish me luck." I did, kissing her cheek. I kept thinking of how beautiful she was, how she had overcome all her depressions. Her career looked great. She was in love. She was in high spirits. The last flash of white into the elevator and a softly whispered

"Bye" as the door slammed, that was it. I would never see Marilyn again.

We talked on the phone several times when she was back in California. It was the first week in August, and Marilyn was thrilled about seeing José Bolanos soon. She was also "a little scared" about telling him she needed more time to consider his proposal. Once she asked me if I thought Twentieth Century-Fox would change their minds and back out of the movie again. I scolded her for imagining things, and she agreed it was stupid. Otherwise, things seemed fine.

On Saturday, August 4, Marilyn called me in the afternoon. She knew I'd be coming to her apartment to check the mail, dust, and do whatever odd jobs needed to be done. She always wanted her wardrobe in perfect condition for her unplanned visits, and always wanted to be sure there was plenty of champagne in the house. That day, she was full of plans. She wanted to have a "lasagna party" on Labor Day for about forty people. The party was for José Bolanos. She wanted all the people she dealt with in New York—the Strasbergs, lawyers, agents, etc.—to meet him. "Make sure the apartment looks nice, Baby Lamb. I want him to like it. I know he'll like you." She said she was taking it easy, trying to rest up for when *Something's Got to Give* started up again. She felt good. Before she hung up, she said, "Give Joey and Johnny a big, big kiss from Marilyn. And tell them I haven't forgotten Disneyland. See you soon."

The next morning, Sunday, my family went to Mass. When we returned to the apartment, the phone was ringing. My husband answered it. It was one of his friends from work. Suddenly, Joe turned white and hung up the phone without saying a word. He looked at me with the saddest look. "Marilyn is dead."

Before the words could register, the phone rang again. It was a relative with the same news. The phone didn't stop ringing. We still couldn't believe what we were hearing. I put on the radio to look for a news station, but I didn't have to turn the dial at all. There it was—Marilyn Monroe, dead at thirty-six, an apparent suicide from an overdose of sleeping pills.

We didn't take time to cry. Joe and I took our boys to his parents upstairs, who were sitting there weeping. They couldn't believe it either. When we arrived at 444 and rushed into the building, the doorman simply shook his head. "They won't let you up, Lena. They won't let anyone up. If you had only gotten here earlier. . . . I feel terrible."

The doorman was right. Plainclothes policemen were standing guard in the lobby. They wouldn't let anyone into the elevator to go upstairs, except the actual tenants of an apartment. "But I'm Miss Monroe's personal maid," I pleaded. "I've been with her for years. I take care of the apartment while she's away." I didn't know what I would accomplish by going upstairs. My mind wasn't working clearly then, anyway. Whose could? I just felt that Marilyn's house was my responsibility, that I had to take care of things for her. And the thought, the dream raced through my mind, that if I were there . . . she would call. Maybe this whole thing was a nightmare, or a mistake by the press. Maybe she recovered. I had seen her take an overdose by accident once before. I remembered panicking when I saw her on the floor. She looked dead then, yet the doctor arrived and pulled her through. She was happily eating spaghetti in hours. Maybe now it was the same story.

It wasn't. My hopes were shattered by the detectives, or whoever they were. There was absolutely no emotion in their faces. None. Hadn't they seen Marilyn in movies? Hadn't she made them happy? I begged them to let me go up. They just shook their heads. "Orders. No one can go upstairs." My husband tried to explain. The doorman tried. Still, the cold faces, the shaking heads.

Joe and I gave up. In a daze, we walked down to the little park at the end of Fifty-seventh Street. This was where Marilyn and I went to walk her beloved little poodle that Frank Sinatra had given her. It was where she had marveled at the glittering Queensboro Bridge at dusk and at the giant oil tankers that passed by. It was "the most romantic spot" in New York, where she dreamed of strolling arm in arm with Joe DiMaggio. Could Marilyn really be gone? At that stage of my life, I had never had to deal with death before. In the short years ahead, my husband would be dead, my parents would be dead. But this was the first time I had lost anyone that close to me. For the first time, I began to sob. Joe and I just sat in the park, on that muggy August day, holding each other and crying, as the big ships sailed by.

The next few days were terrible. We tried several times to get back into the apartment, to no avail. Then the newspapers started coming out, with all the stories and rumors. It seemed to me absolutely impossible that Marilyn could have committed suicide. I had just talked to her. She was happy. She was making plans. She was beautiful. She had everything to live for.

The only possible reason for her being depressed was that something may have gone wrong in her affair with José Bolanos. Yet she had lived with disappointments all her life, both in love and in her career. She had been unhappy, for sure, but had always snapped back. The only time I ever saw her even think about suicide was that night at her window when she had lost Arthur Miller, Yves Montand, and Clark Gable all at almost the same time, though in different ways. She was miserable about her career. She hated being overweight. Yet even then I don't think she was all that serious about jumping. She had admitted how stupid it was. Marilyn liked challenges, and life was too big a challenge for her to back away from it.

As for her death being an accident, Marilyn had been taking pills for as long as I had known her. Only that one time in the past had she taken an overdose by mistake. She was truly sorry for it. No matter how reckless she may have seemed, washing down sleeping pills with champagne, Marilyn knew exactly what her body could take. Within those limits, she was extremely careful. To this day, her death has remained a mystery to me.

And a tragedy. In all the newspaper accounts, the one that made me cry the most was a story with a picture of Joe DiMaggio, the day of Marilyn's funeral in California. He had always come through for her, and he came through again in the end, when for all her fame, she had no one else who would take care of her burial. I could see by the look on his face how tormented he was. If he had only married her again, he must have been thinking. Then he would have been at her side at all times, and nothing could have hurt her. I read how Joe went up to Marilyn's coffin, and kissed her good-bye for the last time, saying "I love you" over and over. No one meant it more than he did.

For me, one of the hardest things of all was trying to explain to my Joey and Johnny that they wouldn't be seeing "their Marilyn" anymore. They understood, and they cried. For all of us, it was a terrible loss. My entire life had revolved around Marilyn for years. Aside from my husband and sons, she was the closest person to me on earth, and my best friend. She always said, "Baby Lamb, I need you." Of course I took care of her, but I also knew that if I ever had any trouble she would be just as quick to take care of me.

I never went back inside 444. Yet for weeks after Marilyn's death, I would walk by on the other side of Fifty-seventh Street and stare up to the thirteenth floor. There was never any sign of life in the apartment. The windows were all closed and dark. I finally had to accept the fact that Marilyn would not be back. But the memories were still there. And the one that has stayed with me most vividly is looking up to that grim thirteenth floor and seeing Marilyn waving and blowing kisses from her bedroom window, wanting to be sure that I was safely on my way home. "Good night, Baby Lamb," I remember her little voice straining against the roar of New York. "Good night, Baby Lamb. See you tomorrow." That was Marilyn—kind, sweet, a woman who knew how to love. That was the Marilyn I'll never forget.